CONTENTS

Foreword
CHAPTER
I   Radiancies of Nature
II   The Radiant Aura
III   A Few Words in Passing
IV   Varied Radiancies
V   Radiancies of Individuality
VI   Conflicting Radiancies
VII   Radiancies of Fear
VIII   The Radiancy of Rebuke
IX   What I Would Radiate to the Wrong Doer
X   The Radiancies of Toleration
XI   Out of Door Radiancies
XII   Radiancies of Joy, Inspiration, and Serenity
XIII   Radiancies of the Will
XIV   Radiancies of Cheerfulness
XV   Radiancies of Moral Courage
XVI   Radiancies of Content and Discontent
XVII   Radiancies of Sincerity
XVIII   Radiancies of Service
XIX   Radiancies of Humor
XX   Radiancies of the "Eternal Now"
XXI   Radiancies of Extremes
XXII   Absorption in Relation to Radiation

FOREWORD

From the standpoint of religion the lives of "good" men and women may be divided into two great classes, viz., those who do no active wrong, whose conduct is based upon the "thou shalt nots" of the Bible, the law, and society, and those whose every thought is to do some active good.

I am far more interested in the latter than the former class. I am not content simply to forego doing wrong. I want to *do*, to *be*. Hence when the idea of *Living a Radiant Life* took hold of me, it sank deep, and is now part of my inner self. It was natural, therefore, that I should seek to formulate my thoughts as to what I desired to radiate. This seeking soon taught me that I already was a radiant being; every thought, every act, every word written or spoken was a radiant act, having its influence for good or evil upon my fellows, and that, therefore, I must decide speedily what I wanted to avoid radiating, and that which I would radiate.

The following pages are some of the results of my earnest cogitations, deliberations, reflections, and decisions. Consequently they partake strongly of personal preachments applied to myself. They may be regarded as a record of personal aspirations and longings, of spiritual hopes, of living prayers, and desires. And they are purposely written in the personal form in the sincere hope that they will help others to put into similar form their own half-formed thoughts, desires, and aspirations.

This book is not offered as a complete manual of life. It is merely a suggestion to others of the larger, wider, better, nobler thing they may do for themselves. It is my desire to arouse thought, to stimulate ardent longings for something beyond the gratification of the senses, to lead my readers to strive more earnestly for unselfish living, and to encourage them in their endeavors to find, realize, and live those spiritual truths which redeem human beings from their mortal inheritance of imperfection.

The main test of any system of religion or code of life is: Does it work? If it is not practical; applicable to all the events of daily life; enabling one to cope with problems as they arise; making one more helpful to mankind, less selfish, less censorious, less vain, less proud, less obstinate, less cruel, less thoughtless, less despondent; and, on the other hand, exciting and stimulating one to be more humane, more tender and compassionate with sinning humanity, more humble and ready to learn, more amenable to the suggestions of the wise and good, more kind, more considerate, more generous, more noble, more aspiring, then, indeed, has it proven itself to be a broken reed, instead of a tried staff upon which one may lean.

No longer to me is religion a question of "Thou shalt not." The "don'ts" of life are of far less importance than the "dos." He whose life is occupied with doing good has little time or thought for doing harm. Christ's method of living was positive and active, rather than negative and passive. He *went about, doing good*. He said: "*Do* unto others as ye would have them do unto you." He taught love in action: Love your enemies, bless them that curse you, do good to them that hate you, and pray for them which despitefully use you, and persecute you.

Hence I earnestly hope that every one of the following pages will contain some helpful thought for all who are seeking the more perfect life; and also for those who are sitting in the darkness of discouragement, under the depressing temptation to regard life as a "failure." There is no man living, no matter how low in body, mind, or soul, but can be helped into happiness; no woman so utterly lost to all good who may not live to feel the sprouting of angel wings because of the birth within her soul of helpful, unselfish love.

Goethe's cry was for "more light," and as life comes with light in the material world, so light and life are inseparably connected in the mental and spiritual world. There is no real darkness in life. There may be a temporary withdrawal of solar light, but we know that as surely as all the days of the past have dawned, so the sun will shine again to-morrow. And through all the seeming mists of doubt, fear, and pain the true spiritual light forever shines to give immortal life. Let us take Life then as God's gift, and as we progress daily to a more perfect expression of freedom from all that would wrongfully enthrall us, let us seek diligently to "let our light shine" upon those around who seem to live in the shadows.

I would come, in these pages, as the glorious sun, bringing warmth, healing, and purification. I would come as the stimulating breeze that vivifies and refreshes—the breeze that has its birth on the vast Pacific where all impurities are scrubbed out of it in a thousand miles of storms, then floats gently over the orange and lemon groves, the rose gardens and violet beds, the sweet scented blossoms of ten thousand times ten thousand shrubs of California; then, laden with sweet odors and charged with the bromine and ozone of the ocean, climbs over the steep Sierran heights and becomes cool and filtered through the vast pine and juniper forests, and adds the balsams of health and strength, distilled from a million trees and shrubs, ere it falls to the desert and is there rendered aseptic and antiseptic. Like such a health-laden breeze would I come to weary men and women, tired and exhausted with the battle of life, sick of its complexities and frivolities, longing for spiritual as well as physical health, and seeking the happiness that comes alone when we live for the happiness of others.

My desire is to send forth a message that will bless body, mind, and soul, just as a triple song, whose melodies blend in perfect harmony, carries healing, strength, and inspiration. For he indeed is thrice blessed who knows the joy of life in its threefold manifestation, who has a body that is vigorous and healthy, a mind alert and active, quick to observe and reflect, to discern and classify, and a soul whose emotions and aspirations are ever to help, encourage, comfort, and purify humanity.

The conditions for such a life are in the "Everywhere" waiting to be born into the "Here," and God's time is *now*.

Many of these chapters originally appeared in the pages of *Physical Culture Magazine*, and to my good friends, its editor and founder, Bernarr Macfadden, and the present editor, John Brennan, I tender my cordial thanks for the privilege of reprinting which they have generously accorded.

George Wharton James

Pasadena, Calif.

PRAYER

OH, ALMIGHTY GOD, Thou radiant source of all power, life and love, Thou free giver of sun and earth, clouds and wind, flowers and trees, fruits and birds, bees and butterflies, work and play, tenderness and unselfishness, sympathy and love, so fill us with Thyself that we shall become radiant beings like Thyself. Make us innocent as little children, simple as the young animals of the hills and fields, beautiful in soul as are the flowers, heaven-aspiring as are the trees, soothing as are the gentle breezes of night, warming as is the sun, fluid to meet all needs as water, restful as night, eager for work as the dawn, joyous in all life as the birds, and thankful for labor as the busy bees. Give us the needy to bless, the loveless to love, the sinful to stimulate and encourage to goodness, purity, and truth, the orphan to father, the degraded to uplift, and at the same time the wise to be our teachers and the serene to lead us into peace. Be Thou our Constant Vision, longing and aspiration—nay, be Thou our never-failing companion, counselor and friend. So shall we become radiant, true children of Thine, possessed of Thy likeness and radiating the glory and beauty of Thyself.

—Amen.

CHAPTER I

THE RADIANCIES OF NATURE

Everything in Nature is radiant. Use the term in its broad sense and there is nothing to which it does not apply. The sun radiates light and heat, and without it life would be impossible. The moon radiates light, but practically no heat. Its light is reflected and of an entirely different character from that of the sun, so that no one ever mistakes the one for the other. The stars have a light all their own which they, though so many millions of miles away from us, radiate in varying intensities. And many of these stars are so individualistic in their radiancies that each one, though perfect, is different from each other one, and may readily be detected by its own peculiarities. Every flower that grows, from the night-blooming cereus on the desert to the most perfect amaryllis developed by Burbank, radiates its own colors, odors, and general appearance. One familiar with them may close his eyes and detect in a moment, by the odor of each—the violet, rose, lily, cosmos, verbena, and a thousand others, and there are those whose olfactory nerves are highly sensitive who can discern, by smell alone, the varieties of each flower.

Every species of tree radiates its own qualities, so that, to the student, they become growingly wonderful in what they give out. A distinguished botanist whom I know is so familiar with the radiancies of the various pines of the Pacific Slope that he can sketch and perfectly describe the complete tree as soon as he sees the cone, or, blindfolded, smells its odor.

Every rock has its own radiancies of color, texture, weight, and density. One of John Ruskin's most useful and beautiful books is his *Ethics of the Dust*, and those who have not read it should do so to understand how many things a wise and good man has felt radiated from the rocks.

Shakspere felt the potency of this truth or he would never have written that he saw "tongues in trees; books in the running brooks; sermons in stones, and good in everything."

Every landscape radiates its own personality. Some are quietly pastoral, as the valleys in Connecticut. The prairies of Illinois, Iowa, and Nebraska are wide and impressive; the wastes of the Colorado Desert are vast and appalling; the varied colorings of the Painted Desert are weird and startling. The orange, lemon, and other orchards of Southern California delight the senses, the forests of the north and the High Sierras stir the soul by their expansiveness, and the groves of Big Trees overpower by their height and size. The ocean is restless and resistless; the stars pitiless at times, soothing at others. Each scene, whether pastoral, picturesque, wild, rugged, grand, or weird, has its peculiar radiancies, and some scenes possess many qualities, all of which are felt or perceived by the sensitive onlooker. For instance, as one stands on the rim of the Grand Canyon he feels the radiancies of overwhelming vastness, profound depth, far-reaching length, expansive width, vivid and extraordinary coloring, bizarre and strange carvings, and, in the lower depths of the Inner Gorge, where flows the solemn and sullen Colorado, a strangeness and mystery found nowhere else in the known world.

In his *Kreutzer Sonata*, Tolstoi contends that certain music radiates damning influences, and though I do not agree with him (perhaps because I have never felt or seen such evil), his attitude of mind serves as a further illustration of my proposition. We all are aware of certain radiancies of certain kinds of music, even though unaccompanied with words. The *Dead March in Saul*; the *Threnody* in Bach's Passion Music; the *Death of the King* in Grieg's *Peer Gynt*, and Chopin's *Funeral March*, all radiate the solemnity and sadness of death, while Sousa's various marches, Chopin's *March Militaire*, and a hundred other similar compositions radiate the arousement either of active life or passionate war. The *Glorias* of Mozart and Pergolesi, and Handel's *Hallelujah Chorus* speak—even though the words are unheard—of the joy of the world at the Savior's birth, and the *Requiems* of Verdi, Bach, and Gounod of the sadness of soul felt at His cruel death.

Every picture radiates the spirit of its artist at the period of creation, and every piece of music the influences that overpower the soul of the composer; and even every piece of furniture radiates to some extent the spirit of the age in which it was created, or the animating spirit of its creator.

It should not be overlooked that, although these radiant properties are possessed for all persons alike, they are not discerned by all alike. All people are not equally receptive, equally sensitive, equally apperceptive. Human beings are like soil—some is stony ground and the seed takes no root, other is thorny, and the seeds, springing up, are choked, other still is good ground and bears fruit, some thirty, some sixty, some an hundred fold. In other words the state of our own responsiveness determines the effect upon us of the radiancy of the objects with which we come in contact.

The quartz picked up from a ledge may be full of valuable mineral, but to the ignorant it is "a piece of rock and nothing more."

The ordinary traveler on the desert sees a large black beetle. Knowing nothing of beetles, it is to him "only a bug." But the scientific entomologist, seeing the same beetle, is carried away with delight, for he recognizes the rare *Dinapate Wrightii*, one of the least seen and most rare of American beetles.

Most travelers seeing the cactuses of the desert note but a few varieties, but the trained observer revels in hundreds of differences in *mammillaria*, *opuntias*, *echinocactuses*, and *agave*.

Some see no beauty in them, some delight in their many and diverse charms; to some their thorns are hideous and repulsive, to others both interesting and beautiful in their arrangement and design.

According to our receptivity do these objects of Nature affect us—some in one way, some another. The more sensitive our minds and souls are to what they perceive, the more we receive, absorb, gain, and, therefore, the more we in turn radiate to others, but we must remember that the character and quality of that which we receive will be reflected, therefore it is necessary to be constantly in that attitude of mind which is receptive to good only.

CHAPTER II

THE RADIANT AURA

Swedenborg, who was one of the most eminent of scientists and engineers, as well as the founder of the religious system that bears his name, asserted that various "aura" surrounded all living beings, and that the mental or spiritual state radiates, just as light and heat radiate from the sun, and cold from the snow. When one was angry, he said, he gave out the aura of anger which enveloped him as a cloud. Hatred had its aura, as well as love, sympathy, purity, impurity, kindliness, charity, jealousy, courage, justice, and the like.

He also asserted that, to those who were simple, natural, and unspoiled by false reasoning—those who were spiritually inclined—these varied aura were clearly perceptible, and were as certainly felt or seen as were heat, cold, whiteness, blackness by the senses.

Rudyard Kipling bases his story, "They," which appeared some years ago in *Scribner's Magazine*, upon this statement of Swedenborg's, and in this light it becomes an extra fascinating story to read.

A great modern French scientist has made many exhaustive studies of these aura, and claims to have photographed them.

In the Panama-Pacific Exposition, one of the exhibits contained a series of interesting pictures, or diagrams, which purported to be exact representations of the various aura of people under different mental conditions. In an article on this subject, written by a well-known authority, we are told that:

> It is not around the human body alone that an aura is to be seen; a similar cloud of light surrounds or emanates from animals, trees, and even minerals, though in all these cases it is less extended and less complex than that of man.

The occultists assert that the aura is extremely complex in its character, in other words, that there are several aura superposed one upon the other. The first appearance is of a luminous cloud, extending some eighteen inches or two feet from the body, assuming a somewhat oval shape. Careful study, however, reveals that this first appearance is resolvable into several component parts, or separate aura, of different degrees of tenuity, and, apparently, superposed. Five of these have been defined. The first, or most material, is that pertaining to the physical body. In a state of health this is composed of separate, orderly, and nearly parallel lines, which radiate from the body in every direction.

When one suffers from disease the lines in the neighborhood of the part affected become erratic, and radiate less actively but in the wildest confusion, or, if the whole body be affected, all the lines are consequently erratic.

For a long time it was not known what kept these lines straight and approximately parallel in the case of the healthy person, until a second radiating aura was discovered. This comes from a healthy body in pulsating waves, with such vigor as to compel the rigidity of the health lines. These waves may be compared to the pulsations of the heated air which rise from the ground on a very hot day. Baron Reichenbach made experiments with certain sensitives who declared they could see these radiations, and he called them "the magnetic flame."

When these "waves" come from a sickly or weakly body they not only lose power, but seem to give a confused direction to the health lines.

Many observations also have led to the conclusion that when the lines are kept straight by the force of the pulsating waves from a healthy and vigorous body, "it seems to be almost entirely protected from the attack of evil physical influences, such as germs of disease—such germs being repelled and carried away by the outrush of the life-force: but when from any cause—through weakness, through wound or injury, through over-fatigue, through extreme depression of spirits, or through the excesses of an irregular life—an unusually large amount of vitality is required to repair damage or waste, within the body, and there is consequently a serious diminution in the quantity radiated, this system of defense becomes dangerously weak, and it is comparatively easy for the deadly germs to effect an entrance."

The third aura is that which expresses one's desires—a kind of mirror in which every feeling, every desire, every thought almost, of the personality is reflected. This changes constantly, in some people, accordingly as they are swayed by their impulses. Its colors, brilliancy, rate of pulsations, alter from moment to moment, or minute to minute. "An outburst of anger will charge the whole aura with deep-red flashes on a black ground; a sudden fright in a moment will change everything to a mass of ghastly livid gray."

Connected with this, and yet, seemingly, of a separate character, are the radiations of the aura that express the progress of the personality into higher and better appreciation of the things of mind and spirit. The more intellectual and spiritual one becomes the more steady and beautiful are the colors and radiations of this aura, and the variations and distressing manifestations of the evil desires of the third aura become less apparent and distinct.

The fifth aura is the highest at present discernible. It manifests the spiritual development of the individual and is of almost inconceivable delicacy and beauty. It seems to be a cloud of living light—the word cloud being used for want of a better term.

In the concrete examples of aura that were presented at the Exposition, that which radiated from a wise mother showing her protective love for her infant, was in the form of outspread wings of a beautiful rosy tint, the wings held together at the articulations by a sheaf-like mass of golden yellow.

Selfish ambition, sudden fear, explosive anger, selfishness, grasping animal affection, greed, jealousy, jealousy mixed with anger, gloom, murderous hatred, were all displayed in peculiar, hideous, and repulsive forms and colors.

Pure, radiating affection, on the other hand, was represented in the form and color of a round body exhaling rays as from a rosy sun. Strange to say, though I had never read anything explicit upon this subject before, I had always conceived of pure affection as giving forth radiations of this exact appearance.

Whether this "occult" explanation of the radiation of aura be a true one or not, it serves to give one a beautiful conception, viz., that every soul may strive so to live within that he sheds upon his fellows glorious rays of light, serenity, warmth, comfort, blessing, joy, happiness that help them to the attainment of like felicities.

In the earlier part of this chapter Swedenborg's assertion will be recalled that those who were unspoiled, real children of Nature, could actually perceive these aura, and that their acts were guided or influenced by them just as ours are by the perceptions of our five senses.

When I began to visit the Hopi Indians in Northern Arizona, who celebrate that wonderfully thrilling religious ceremony known as the Snake Dance, I found that their lives conformed exactly to this aura assumption. They handle deadly rattlesnakes with fearlessness, putting small ones into their mouths so that nothing but their heads protrude, and larger ones, up to five feet in length, in their teeth, head on one side of the mouth, the writhing, wriggling body on the other. Young boys, from three to six and ten years of age—neophytes of the Antelope Clan, which, with the Snake Clan, has charge of this ceremonial prayer for rain—hold these snakes during a part of the ceremony with an indifferent carelessness that is appalling to most onlookers. On the other hand those who are alive to the dangers attending the handling of snakes assert positively that the reptiles must have their fangs removed, as otherwise they would bite, and either cause death or dangerous sicknesses.

Yet both classes of observers are in error. The snakes are not handled carelessly, nor are their fangs removed. Apparent carelessness is often the result of years of training, the ease and readiness that come with much experience. Fearlessness is another result of experience and knowledge. But, once in a while, a member of the Snake Clan is afraid, and at such times he is not allowed to dance. In this exclusion is a strong suggestion that the Hopis fully believe that not only do the aura of our mental and spiritual states surround us, but that even to the lower animals they are as perceptible as light, heat, and cold. It may be true that the truly occult, or clairvoyant, by pure and simple living, return to the clarity of spiritual perception of the child and the lower animals, and they likewise see and understand. In the case of the snakes, the Hopis believe that if a dancer is afraid it makes the snake afraid. In other words, the reptile sees or discerns the "fear aura," and, at once, its own fear is awakened. When afraid it assumes the defensive, for that is its only mode of protection. It coils ready to strike, and rattles in warning: Beware!

On the other hand, when the dancer is unafraid and handles the reptile in the true Hopi spirit, viz., as his *Elder Brother*—for, according to Hopi mythology, the Snake Clan originates with the Snake Mother, and therefore all members of it are younger brothers to all snakes—the aura of friendliness and brotherly kindliness surrounds him, which, being perceived by the snake, it is at once soothed and allows itself to be handled with restfulness and assurance of safety. And in the thirteen times that I have witnessed the Snake Dance (and several times been privileged to see and take part in the secret ceremonials of the underground chambers where the snakes are handled and washed), only twice have I known any one to be bitten.[A]

CHAPTER III

A FEW WORDS IN PASSING

Perhaps the majority of human beings do not really *live*: they merely *exist* for a time in the flesh and for the flesh. And as all are constantly reminded that such existence is temporary and fleeting it is a very common belief that only in youth can one "have a good time." Old age is dreaded because we have been taught to expect a greater or lesser degree of decrepitude, pain, and physical disability when we shall pass the so-called "Bible-limit" of three-score years and ten, and, therefore, we anticipate losing our powers of enjoyment. Fathers and mothers encourage their children to "make the most of their youth," and to "get all out of life they can while they have the opportunity," thus fostering and cultivating a high state of nervous tension in young people that is demoralizing in every way.

I believe this attitude is wrong, and yet I believe fully in "having a good time." I believe God intended that all living beings should be happy, and that it is possible to order our lives—our habits, actions, thoughts, desires, and ambitions—so that every conscious hour of every day will be full of real joy. I believe in the buoyancy, the happiness, the radiancy, the perfection of life. Browning expresses my thought in *Rabbi Ben Ezra*, and in *Saul*. In the latter he says:

> Oh, our manhood's prime vigor! No spirit feels waste,
> Not a muscle is stopped in its playing nor sinew unbraced,
> Oh, the wild joys of living!...
> How good is man's life, the mere living, how fit to employ
> All the heart and the soul and the senses forever in joy!

And in *Rabbi Ben Ezra* he says:

> Grow old along with me!
> The best [of life] is yet to be.

And why should not old age be the best part of life? Does experience count for nothing? Can we not learn as the years roll along? Do we grow more foolish as we grow old? If so it might be advisable to let the facetious suggestion of the celebrated Dr. Osier be carried out in order that all men might be chloroformed at the age of fifty. If, however, history and experience teach us that the intellectual faculties and reasoning powers of a man in normal health do not decrease with age, let us protest vigorously against the false and injurious statement that youth is the best part of life, and let us advocate that we should all possess greater mental and spiritual ability at ninety than at thirty, with physical powers of endurance ample for every need.

It is recorded in the Bible that many of the ancients lived to be several hundred years old, and some of them were vigorously active at great age. We are told that Cornaro lived many years more than a century, and I have personally known Indians of great physical power and keen mentality who were over one hundred years old. Doubtless all are familiar with instances of great mental and physical ability at an advanced age, and this is an encouragement for us to believe that health and happiness and usefulness are not confined to the early decades of human life. My words, therefore, are not addressed merely to the young, but to those of all ages, for it is never too late to gain more of that mental health which strengthens body, mind, and soul—the real life which is manifested in love, joy, and all goodness, and constantly radiates life-giving qualities. Radiancy is a condition of all life, as I use the term in these pages. No person can rightly live and retain within himself that which he possesses in abundance. We must give out in order to live. Christ never spake a truer word than when He declared: "He that loveth his life shall lose it." Those who are so careful to keep all of their lives for themselves, who never give of themselves to others, who know nothing of the joy of self-sacrifice, of service, of helpfulness—these people defeat the very object of their selfishness by losing that which they are so determined to retain. On the other hand, "he that hateth his life in this world shall keep it unto life eternal." Or, as Joaquin Miller exquisitely and forcefully puts it in his unequaled couplet:

> For all you can hold in your dead, cold hand,
>   Is what you have given away.

So, then, radiation of the good of ourselves becomes an essential condition in itself of real life. This law of radiation is apparent everywhere in life. For, consciously or unconsciously, willingly or unwillingly, each man and woman radiates what is within. The moment you come into the presence of some men you feel their uprightness, their integrity, their truth. Other men impress you in a moment as untruthful, dishonorable, and unreliable. Some radiate confidence, so that the weak and uncertain rely upon them; others the hesitancy and fear of incertitude. Others are radiant centers of conceit and overweening self-esteem, which is an entirely different radiancy from that of self-confidence and true self-reliance combined with good sense and modesty. Some people radiate gluttony, others drunkenness, others impurity, others dishonesty. You have not been in the presence of some persons five minutes before you feel that they radiate "Every man has his price." It is a great temptation when I come into the presence of such people to ask, "What is your price?" and then myself to give the answer: "Thirty cents, and it is twenty-nine cents too dear."

During a recent little outing trip I could not help witnessing the varying radiancies of a friend and the thirty students that he invited to accompany us. One young man was full of physical energy, good nature, and helpfulness. With keen eye he was prompt to notice any failure to keep up in the less strong of the girls, and, with jollity and jest, but with real consideration and helpfulness, he aided the weaklings whenever and wherever possible. One of the girls radiated an abundance of joyous healthfulness that made it a pleasure to watch her. Another was a thoughtless go-ahead young miss, who led a large part of the group a mile or two out of the way. Two of the girls were fault-finders, three were radiators of efficient initiative when time came for preparing lunch, and half a dozen were "ready to help," but had no idea how to go to work until directed by some one else. One was able to determine somewhat the real character of the persons by that which they radiated. Of course, that is not always a sure guide, for one may pretend, or affect the possession of qualities that are not inherent. Yet if we lived the true life and never dulled the keenness of our sense perceptions, we should be like the animals and able to rely absolutely upon what we felt of the radiancies of others. Who has not seen the keen readiness of a horse to "sense" the mental condition of the man who was driving him? Suppose two men sit in the buggy. One holds the lines, but is unused to driving and especially nervous in a city. He radiates nervousness and fear, uncertainty and hesitancy. The horse feels these radiancies and himself is nervous, fretful, fearful, hesitant, and uncertain. Seeing this, his friend takes the lines. Almost instantly, though the horse has "blinders" on and cannot possibly know by any ordinary sense perception that a change has taken place in his driver, he calms and quiets down, and goes ahead without further fear, hesitancy, or nervousness.

With dogs, every one knows that to be afraid of a barking, yelping, aggressive cur is to invite him to bite you. But if you advance upon him boldly and without any fear he will retreat in snarling dismay, and if you make a bold dash at him he turns tail like the veriest coward and runs. In my many visits to Indian villages and camps I have tested this again and again. I have had a dozen dogs run out as if they would tear me to pieces. Had I turned and run there is no doubt that, unless their owners had interfered, I should have been bitten. But, knowing the nature of the ill-bred curs of the Indians, I advanced boldly upon them, kicking to left and right, if the animals were more than usually persistent, and invariably following into his own place of refuge the animal that seemed to be the leader, and there giving him one or two sharp blows or decisive kicks. The result was always the same. So long as I stayed in that camp I was never bothered again. They readily and quickly understood the radiancy of boldness and that of kindness when they ceased their fierce aggressiveness, and never pestered me again.

This same radiant power of others is often recognized by lawless men and by criminals. A fearless woman can go into places of great danger with absolute safety, and a fearless and honest officer can arrest the most desperate and dangerous men far more easily than can a dozen fearful and dishonest ones.

Thus it will be apparent that:

Every person, animal, and thing, consciously or unconsciously, willingly or unwillingly, radiates good or evil.

As human beings we radiate that which we possess, or that which possesses us, and we influence those with whom we come in contact by our radiancies.

The questions, then, that every true-hearted man and woman must, and will, ask are: "Am I radiating good or evil? If evil, why? If good, am I radiating as much as I might and should?"

For myself I want every man and woman I meet or shake hands with, to feel that I am physically strong, healthy, and vigorous; that I have vigor and health of mind; that I think for myself, rather than accept the opinions of others, and that in character, in spirit, in soul, I am healthy, vigorous, sincere, pure, true; that my emotions, my aspirations, my ambitions are noble and upward. I want to radiate spiritual health. Do you?

CHAPTER IV

VARIED RADIANCIES

Man is a part of Nature, but he is more than that which we mean by the words, "mere Nature." He is Nature plus. There is given to him more than is possessed by sun or flower. He has within him that spirit which renders him nearer the divine than sun or flower. Mind and *soul* make him a superior being. Hence it is the divine plan that he should radiate in his enlarged sphere as the sun and flower do in theirs.

Unfortunately, while we are in the body, our imperfect and evil qualities are radiated as well as our good. This is our misfortune, and should be our distress. For certainly every true man and woman would desire to radiate only truth, purity, sincerity, courage, good judgment, self-control, stamina, or perseverance in good endeavor, energy, love of knowledge, mental capacity, justice, tact, ability, executive power, regard for the rights of others, kindliness, individuality, self-reliance, readiness to avail one's self of the wisdom of others, self-dependence, attractiveness of person, companionable qualities, good manners, good taste in dress, attractiveness of mind and soul (this as differentiated from mere attractiveness of person), cheerfulness, optimism, and altruism, readiness to see and have faith in the good of others, and good humor.[B]

Who could ever resist the radiating influences of a Mark Tapley, such as Dickens so vividly pictures? Such radiancies penetrate so deeply that nothing can obliterate them. The greater the cause for wretchedness and misery, the greater the opportunity to "come out strong" and show that his spirit of cheerfulness was greater than any untoward circumstance. Happy is that man or woman who gives out such radiancies, and blessed are those who come in contact with them.

Certain men and women radiate gloom and the abnormal recognition of their physical ills. You greet them with a cheery "Good morning" and they respond with an explicitly detailed wail of their ailments. Their rheumatism is "so bad," and their liver is out of order. Their backache is worse, and their headache is "simply frightful."

Brooding over their pains and aches has magnified them so that they overshadow all things else in the universe. An earthquake and fire that destroy a great city are of less importance to them than the recital of their own woes.

How different the cheery radiancies of the happy man—like Dickens's Cheeryble Brothers—who gives out breezy healthfulness on every hand. The clasp of the hand radiates physical vigor that in itself is a tonic to the body; their bright and cheerful words brace up the mind; and their God-like optimism and altruism lift up the soul so that—above the mists and fogs of mortal error—we see God and enjoy His smile.

Some persons radiate selfishness. I was riding in the train the other day. A woman had two whole seats, that is, her suit case took up one and she sat on the other. The car was filled with people; every other seat occupied. At the next station eight or ten people came aboard, and all found places by the side of some one else, except one woman. Walking down to where the whole seat was occupied by the suit case she asked the owner if she might have the seat. "I suppose if there's no other you can have it!" she replied in a surly and gruff tone. God save us from radiating selfishness like this!

It is an almost daily occurrence to see a tired man or woman get upon a street car and no one makes a move to give a seat, when that is all it needs —just a little sitting nearer. This may be thoughtlessness, but all the same it is selfishness; a forgetfulness of the sweet privilege of helping others, no matter who.

The wife of Sir Bartle Frere once sent a servant to meet her husband, who was just returning from Africa, an illness preventing her from going. The man did not know Sir Bartle, and he asked for a description. "The only description you will need," said his wife, "is this: Look out for a fine-looking man who is helping some poor woman carry a baby, or a basket, or a load." And, sure enough, when the train arrived he found the distinguished diplomat, the great statesman, helping a poor laundry woman carry her large basket of soiled linen. Ah, Sir Bartle, I greet you a nobleman indeed, for you have radiated unselfishness, thoughtful helpfulness, to me, and through me, to others, and thus out and on forever.

Some persons radiate cynical distrust of their fellows. "There are no honest men!" "I wouldn't believe in the integrity of that man under oath." "Believe every man dishonest until he has proven himself honest, and even then, watch out. He'll be liable to catch you if you nap." "Do others as they would do you, but do it first," said David Harum. "A profession of religion is but a cloak for evil." "If your bank cashier is a Sunday-school Superintendent, watch him!" "Look out for the man who has no open vices."

These are the catchwords of this class of persons. How pernicious and evil are their radiancies.

Commend the fearless bravery of a Roosevelt, the unpopular decisions of an upright judge, the single-heartedness of a labor leader, the integrity of a railroad official, and you are met with the sneer of the lip, the cynical glance of the eye and the scornful words: "He's only waiting for his price."

Far rather would I meet the converse of this cynic in the optimist who believes that every man is as good as he professes to be. For such an abounding faith in mankind, freely radiated, has the effect of calling forth faithfulness, and thus creating what it expects.

I know a woman who, though abundant in good works and very kindly in some ways, who seeks opportunities for helping the helpless and distressed, yet, when others fail to measure up to her own standard, is harsh, censorious, bitter, and fault-finding to a degree that many find it impossible to listen to her without distress. Thus her kindly deeds are overlooked and ignored and she radiates to a large degree discomfort, unrest, and irritation.

At our house we were once privileged to know a woman, recently widowed, who had a crippled and almost helpless son of about a dozen years of age. When her husband was alive she was the president of the leading woman's club in her State and also the president of the State Federation of Women's Clubs—a woman of executive ability and strong mentality, though shy and unassuming.

Her husband was a well-known Governmental specialist in plants, trees, etc., and she had aided him, in some of his investigations, to such a degree that she was almost as expert as he. Unfortunately she was afflicted with deafness. When her husband died she was left with only a few hundred dollars. Her deafness prevented her taking any of the positions her mental qualifications so eminently fitted her to fill. Her crippled son must be cared for. Bravely and fearlessly, yet cautiously and studiously, she determined to make the living for herself and son. She bought a small ranch, planted it out in vegetables and small fruit, and, as the crops matured, personally drove to town and marketed them. Yet with all this arduous work and care she found time and strength to read to her boy (whose eyesight was poor), to help him in his studies and sympathize with him in his boyish endeavors to accomplish something as an electrician. There was no complaining, no weeping at her hard fate—simply a brave recognition of her position and a cheerful facing of the responsibilities thrust upon her. The sorrow and pain she felt keenly, yet one saw no sign of suffering. One day she came to our home and would have said nothing of her difficulties had we not pressed her to tell us about her affairs. She made no claim for sympathy because of the way Fate had tried her, but when we offered it, in our simple and unpretentious fashion, she accepted it in as simple and unaffected a way. Her uncomplaining courage, her fearless grappling with the hard problems of life, radiated inspiration to all who came in close enough contact to know her. We were all benefited and blessed by her presence and the helpful radiancies she shed upon us.

Here is another case. We are honored and blessed with the friendship of the widow of an Episcopal clergyman. For over twenty-five years she and her husband lived in marital oneness, and seven boys and girls crowned their happiness. She awoke one morning to find him dead by her side. The shock was crushing and few would have blamed her had she been incapacitated for a while by its sudden awfulness. But in an instant she leaped to meet her burdens and responsibilities. Religion was real to her. Her husband was with God. He was safe. It was her duty now to be both father and mother to her children. A struggle then began which is as pathetic as it is heroic. I have watched every battle and known the courage, the patience, the fidelity, the failures, the successes. A house, partially built with funds contributed by friends, was eventually lost to the mortgagees. The oldest daughter, after years of brave and cheerful struggle with poverty and ill-health, passed away. A few years later, within a week of each other, two of the noble sons, one about twenty-seven years of age, the other nineteen, the former the most Christ-like youth I have ever known, also died. Then the third daughter, happily married, died after giving birth to her third child, and, in a short time, owing to some strange perversion which it is hard to understand, the son-in-law took it into his head to refuse the grandmother the privilege of seeing the children. The one remaining son, who had studied with honors at the California State University, went East to complete his special studies at Yale, suddenly collapsed mentally, and was cared for for a long time in an Eastern hospital.

Think of the tragedies and sorrows thus crowded into one life in the short space of twenty years! Yet during the whole of this time, though I have been as close to the family as though I were an uncle or older brother; though all their affairs have been regularly and fully unfolded to me, there have been absolutely no wailings, no repinings, no complaints, and only the few tears that it is a relief to let flow when loving hearts sympathize. Instead, this brave woman, her heart fortified by an abiding faith in and love for God, has been "abundant in good works." She is the "right hand support of her clergyman," and every poor and needy person in the parish has experienced her practical interest, help, and loving sympathy. Though unable personally to contribute of material things, she has interested those who could, and has thus made her sympathy practical and genuine. Her home for many years was the rallying ground for homeless young men—mainly, of course, belonging to her own church—who have been immeasurably blessed by her motherly sympathy, loving counsel, and helpful advice.

There radiates from her and her family a living belief in the goodness of God, an assurance that "all things work together for good to them that love God," and that faith in God produces a living courage, and daily strength, a power to overcome affliction that is nigh to the marvelous. To some it might appear almost like indifference; yet those who know, as I do, can testify to the keenness of the inner feeling, the longing for the companion whose dear presence was so awfully and suddenly removed, the heart-crushing losses of children, the terrible burden of the mental disturbance of the brilliant-minded and noble-hearted son. To be brave, cheerful, helpful to others, and strong to do under such burdens is to prove one's self possessed of the power of the living God. It is the radiation of the truths of religion more potent than all the arguments of all the theologians of all the ages.

Still another case comes to mind while I write. It is of a woman who braved disinheritance by a stern father in order that she might marry the man she loved. She came to the United States with him, and on a vineyard in California they struggled happily together, with a poverty that was almost sordid in its piteousness. After two children were born the husband died, leaving the wife with these little ones, together with another child whom she had practically adopted, and a mortgage at heavy rates of interest upon the home place. The house in which they had lived for several years was poor and altogether devoid of comfort, but shortly before the husband's death it had been made comfortable by the addition of several good rooms.

Without a word of complaint this delicately nurtured, refined woman, who, in her English home, had been the organist and director of the choir of a large church, took up the burden of running a California fruit farm. Heavily in debt, interest imperatively demanded every three months, knowing little of the practical working of such a place, she personally took hold and learned. She milked cows night and morning, took them back and forth to pasture, bred calves for the butcher, made butter, raised chickens, drove weary miles summer and winter giving music lessons, and yet kept home more comfortable for her growing brood than does many a woman well provided with funds and help. In time the mortgage was paid off, and a windmill and water tank added to the equipment of the place. The children helped as they grew up, and yet they were kept at school.

When apricots and peaches were ripe I have seen her for days and weeks at a time cutting and pitting them for drying, until a half score or more of tons were lying in their drying trays on the alfalfa. For hours at a time, in the hot sun, she sorted raisins and stacked them up in the sweat-boxes, and did it happily, cheerfully, uncomplainingly, in memory of the husband she so much loved.

Can one come in contact with such a life without feeling its blessed radiancies of courage, energy, triumph over unpleasant circumstances, cheerful doing of disagreeable work, and the power of love to sweeten all things? To know this woman is to be helped, strengthened, and blessed. The bravery of such heroines far surpasses that of much lauded military and naval heroes, and a few such women are worth more to the race, in my judgment, than all the Napoleons, Pompeys, Cæsars, and Nelsons that ever lived.

Certain men impress you with their calm self-reliance. They are not disturbed by precedents or adverse judgments. They do what they deem to be right and refuse to be swerved from the path they have laid out for themselves. Ruskin radiates this influence, so do Carlyle and Browning. Every man who has dared to make innovations, deviate from the "ways of the old," has had to be self-reliant. Every reformer of every age and in every field has had no other staff to lean upon than the assurance of his own soul. Galileo in his astronomical deductions; Savonarola in his criticisms of the existing political conditions; Luther in his fulminations against the evils of the church; Cromwell in his stand against the doctrine of the "divine right of kings"; Jefferson, Washington, and the whole of our fathers, who, according to English *law*, were rebels and revolutionists, in the Declaration of Independence; Lincoln in his war measures and Emancipation Proclamation—all these and a thousand others radiated such self-reliance upon the principles they enunciated and advocated as to convince their followers.

Every political party based upon real principles (rather than upon a desire for spoils), is organized as the result of the radiation of those principles held in the self-reliant hearts of a few men. Every school of thought, in philosophy, theology, medicine, law, ethics, or political economy, is based upon the radiation of ideas from self-reliant men.

Yet there is a marked difference between this quality and that of self-conceit. When Carlyle said of the grammarian who criticised his grammar, "Why, mon, I'd have ye ken that I mak' language for such men as ye to mak' their grammar books from," he stated a fact. He was self-reliant, but not conceited. So with Ruskin, when, in response to my question as to what literature I should read to cultivate a pure style of English, after commenting on the worth of several masters, concluded somewhat as follows: "And there are those who say you should read what I have written, and I agree with them, for I believe I have written more carefully than most men." That was critical self-judgment, not self-conceit. Still we are all more or less familiar with the conceit of ignorance, the assumption of men and women who do not know the mere alphabet of the subjects they profess to be experts on. Recently, on our sleeping car, when a few people got together to sing, one of the passengers, with a self-conceit that was as ludicrous as it was ignorant, spoke of the baritone voice of one of the women and discoursed learnedly upon the bass of the man who was singing tenor.

We have a writer in California who knows so well that he knows, that some of us think he knows "by the grace of God," without study or effort. His whole radiancy is one of cocksure self-conceit.

Who has not felt the radiancy of the miserliness of some men and women! Those who would "squeeze the eagle on a penny until the poor bird screams."

In his *Tom Brown at Rugby*, Hughes shows that Arnold always radiated his full appreciation of all the good in all the boys under his care. Maud Ballington Booth is a wonderful illustration of training to perceive the good radiancies in men and women in whom most others can see and feel only evil.

Is not this a quality of soul to be highly desired? How beautiful, how helpful, how comforting to others long used to feeling that only the evil of them is radiated to others, to feel the sympathy of a large-hearted, pure, beautiful soul which has responded to the weak radiancies of the good that struggles for life within.

For, just as I have shown elsewhere that we must be alert to receive the radiancies of animate and inanimate nature, so must we be receptive to that which our fellow beings radiate. We should train ourselves in receptiveness to that which is good. All prejudice, narrowness, conceit, over self-confidence, cocksureness, tend to ward off the good radiancies of others. There are odors so subtle that the olfactory nerves of most people are incapable of recognizing them. There are notes so refined that ordinary ears cannot hear them, and we are all familiar with the fact that there are infinite depths of space that the largest telescopes fail to penetrate. The expert violinist cherishes his sense of touch that he may not vitiate his playing, and the engraver, the watchmaker, and the workers in a score and one other trades cultivate and preserve high sensitiveness of touch in order that they may become more expert. The piano tuner's ear recognizes variations in the vibrations of the strings he is tuning that most of us fail to appreciate, and the ear of a Theodore Thomas, Carl Muck, Charles Halle, or any other masterly conductor, recognizes fine shades of expression, harmony, and tastefulness in the playing of an orchestra that but few can appreciate. Browning in *Rabbi Ben Ezra* speaks of things that God takes note of in measuring the man's account that men ignore:

> All instincts immature,
> All purposes unsure;
> Thoughts hardly to be packed

> Into a narrow act.
> All I could never be,
> All men ignored in me,
>   This I was worth to God.

We may not be able to discern these "instincts immature," these "facts that break through language and escape," but we can assuredly discipline our minds and souls to see, hear, feel, and touch many beautiful things in our fellows which we too often ignore.

Reader, what are you radiating? I cannot answer that question. Your friends and your enemies may tell in part. You alone can tell all. Sit down some day, many days, and study yourself. Weigh yourself. See how much good you are doing, how much evil. Write out a balance sheet. It will help you in your efforts to know what you most need to seek to radiate in future, and what to avoid radiating.

You surely do not *want* to radiate evil.

You surely *want* to radiate only good.

Is it not better consciously to radiate that which you wish than unconsciously (or thoughtlessly) to radiate that which you do not wish?

As, consciously or unconsciously, we radiate that which is within us, whether good or evil, should we not aim consciously to radiate the best of which we are capable, and thus evidence that we are striving to overcome all the evil that may be within us?

CHAPTER V

RADIANCIES OF INDIVIDUALITY

I want to radiate individuality. I want to be myself and none other. If I see in others things to emulate, things that will more fully make me what I want and ought to be, then emulation becomes a joyful duty—the something in another becomes part of myself through my desire, my emulation, my longing to attain. Hence in the right seeking to be myself I seek also to be like all the good in others which appeals to me. Herein is no destruction of my individuality. It is a perfecting of it. I take what is my own, no matter where or how I find it.

It is so well known as to be trite that men and women are mere sheep. We follow our leaders. We are anything but individual. In religion, in medicine, in law, in speech, in dress, in amusements, in architecture, in literature, in food, in everything, custom and fashion dominate us.

I would radiate a healthy resistance to the dictates of fashion. Why should fashion ride rough-shod over the wisdom of men and women? The hoop-skirt, the stove-pipe collar and hat, the camel's hump of fifteen or twenty years ago that the ladies wore as an extra adornment, the chignon, and a thousand and one other foolish things that once domineeringly dared us to defy them have disappeared. Why should we ever have yielded to them? What is fashion, anyhow? She is a fickle damsel, generally proud of her money, whose good looks are often the result of powder and paint and chalk and rouge instead of good health, vigor, and love. She is a mere flirt, carried away for a few hours with anything as a whim to pass away the time; without heart, feeling, sensibility, brain, or knowledge. Her fads are more likely to be wrong than right, and when right are generally the result of a lapse into sensibility by relinquishing any pretense at thought into the hands of some one who can think for her. Fashion, a heartless, conscienceless, soulless jade whose friendship and favor are a curse, whose flatteries are hollow, insincere, and corrupting, and whose only use for any one or anything lasts merely so long as her own selfish pleasures are attained or desire for novelty satisfied.

Why let fashion dictate what we shall wear? Radiate your distrust of its judgment. Radiate your refusal to submit to its dictates. Radiate your full and calm determination, without argument, to live in your own way. If a certain "style" of dress, which is structural, honest, neat, is suited to you to-day, it is suited to you to-morrow and for all time. Be yourself and *wear that style* regardless of the fluctuations of fashion. Why should fashion say that a man's overcoat this year shall fit him tightly and keep him warm, and next year fit him loosely and send him into the cold, through a storm, shivering and chilled? What sense, what manliness, what dignity, is there in allowing a "fashion-designer" to thus have the opportunity of ruining our health? Let us radiate our positive repudiation of such insane follies, of such sins against our bodies, and in our dress, our food, our social customs, be ourselves in a kindly, unselfish, unobtrusive manner.

Wherever fashion dictates in matters of dress, of personal custom, there you find at once a restricted and "provincial" people. For fashion compels adherence to her silly commands, hence picturesque individuality disappears. A few years ago the clever editor of the New York *Journal* wrote an editorial against men's wearing whiskers. One part of his argument was that the hairs were carriers of disease-germs, and that, therefore, a man with whiskers was dangerous and to be shunned. Thousands of the poor people of New York read and believed this man's preposterous screed, and were thus made unhappy and miserable, and by mental suggestion rendered more liable to the attacks of disease than they would have been had these foolish words never been penned.

It was fashion—not a care for health—that dictated those words. We Americans so love the intellectual conversation and edifying monologues of our barbers that we allow them to dictate to us whether we shall have hair on our cheeks or not, whether we shall have our necks shaved, and how much and whose "restorer" we shall put upon our hair.

I use the barber here merely as a type. He by no means stands alone.

I am determined to radiate a quiet but forceful protest against having my life or that of my fellows dictated to, in purely personal matters, by any one, whether he be priest, doctor, lawyer, barber, or editor. Let each live his own life, within reasonable bounds, and let each *expect* every other to be himself. In nature there are no two things alike, yet fashion would have us *all alike*; and, it might be added, therefore, all foolish.

In seeking for the expression of yourself do not for one moment think it is necessary for you to think out something new, original, startling, or strange. That is not the idea at all. Your life may be *yours*—purely individualistic, and yet everything you do and say and think and feel be as old as the hills. The idea is this. No matter where you get the thoughts from that incite you to action, *make them your own*; *let them become a part of yourself*, then your life will be yours indeed; an expression of your own soul, and not that imitation of another that Emerson so truthfully says is suicide.

But in the radiating of my own individuality I must be so filled with the true spirit of individuality that I shall in no way interfere with that of others. Too often men and women in seeking to be "individual" have seriously trespassed upon the rights, the joys, the comforts of others. This is a fundamental error. The first law of individualism is this: "What I claim for myself I *thereby freely accord* to all others." Note the word "thereby." In the very fact and act of claiming I *thereby* freely recognize *to the utmost* the right of every one else to claim the same right. There is no selfishness in individualism; there are no "special" privileges in its exercise. It is the habit of a few to believe that *they* should have "special" privileges accorded them. True individualism recognizes no such special rights. In *taking* we *give*. In claiming we avow the right of others to claim.

The trouble with mankind is that it has not learned that souls are individuals; that the diversities seen between plants, the differences that exist even between blades of grass, so that there are no two blades exactly alike, is but indicative of the individualism of the human soul. There is a family likeness, for we are all created in God's image, but God is so large, so great, so diverse, in Himself, that each soul is a different image. Hence each soul must be itself and not another. Each soul must develop in its own lines and not in those of others.

The great errors have come in when men have said: "I have found the way of life; it is the only way; all men, therefore, must walk herein." It is a very human error, yet error it certainly is. That Roman Catholicism is "the way" for many human souls no one can question, but that it is "the only way for all human souls" many millions have questioned and doubtless for ever will question. Every church, every creed, every philosophy has those for whom it is "the way," for the time being at least, and it is well that they walk therein. But in thought religion, as in everything else, progress is the law of life, not standing still. In religious thought, as in all life, let us say with our whole souls:

> So welcome each rebuff
> That turns earth's smoothness rough,
> Each sting that bids not sit, nor stand, but go.

Onward, forward, is the cry. The law of evolution has demonstrated that there must ever be the disturbance of the equilibrium on the lower plane in order that there may be the readjustment upon the higher. Every soul that sits still and rests content is retrogressing. There must ever be a godly discontent—a reaching out, a following after, as Paul puts it, if that we may apprehend—take hold of—the things for which Christ Jesus has taken hold of us.

Every soul-field must be plowed and harrowed after each harvest. Crops do not volunteer very often, and a volunteer crop is never so good as one that is carefully prepared for; ground thoroughly nourished, plowed, drained, harrowed, rolled, seeded with the best of seed, watered, weeded, and properly harvested. Is a soul's harvest to be left to chance, while farmers take anxious thought for field-harvests, where only a few dollars' worth of produce are the outcome? Let us be wise for our own souls.

I can only radiate individuality when I am individualistic.

Is there no infallible, certain, sure way of doing things? Of learning things?

I know not what others have found, I only know for myself *that there is but one way, and that is the way of personal test and experience.*

Cardinal Newman, one of the greatest, simplest, purest, and sweetest minds of the last century, had to put his life's guidance into the hands of the church—the Mother Church, to him—the Roman Catholic Church. His piteous cry has voiced the cry of millions of human souls since; souls groping in the dark, seeking for light, desiring above all to *know*.

> Lead, kindly light, amid th' encircling gloom,

>   Lead Thou me on;
> The night is dark, and I am far from home,
>   Lead Thou me on.
> Keep Thou my feet; I do not ask to see
> The distant scene; one step enough for me.

It was his desire to know that led him to write the hymn.

What a profound truth Emerson said when he wrote: "A man should learn to detect and watch that gleam of light which flashes across his mind from within, more than the luster of the firmament of bards and sages. Yet he dismisses without notice his thought, *because it is his*."

The italics are mine. Why will men rely more upon written words than upon the flashes of illuminated truth that come to their own souls? God and His truth are as much for me as for any man. There is as much truth, wisdom, knowledge in the universe for me as for all the wise and learned of all the ages. It is outside of me, waiting to come in, anxious to come in if I will allow it to do so, and yet I allow a Board of Bishops, a College of Medicine, a Bench of Judges to dictate to me as to what of God and His truth I shall receive. While it is my duty and privilege to study reverently all which these people would present to me as the truth, I want to radiate with all the power of my nature my belief that every soul must find truth for itself. There is no patent truth extractor that suits every human need. Conventional thought which professes to express "the truth" is merely man's sign-board to point out to you the way some one else has found truth. Too often, alas, it is used as a restricting bond to tell you beyond which bounds you must not go. Let no man bind you. God is over all and in all. His truth is everywhere. *Seek in spirit and in truth* and you will find,—*for yourself.* But be careful, when you have found for yourself, that you do not make the common mistake of most human beings, and endeavor to force your truth, appropriate and suitable for you, down the mental and spiritual throats of every one else as the appropriate and suitable truth for them. Leave to every other soul the right, the privilege, the joy, the necessity of finding truth for himself, herself. Tell what you have found, if you like, but tell it reverently, as a gift to you, not as a divine light for every one else.

This, therefore, is the individuality I would radiate. I would have the Hindoo, the Hottentot, the Hopi, the Roman Catholic, the Mormon, the

Chinaman, the Methodist all feel that I revere and respect their individuality even as I revere and respect my own. But, further—and here is the important thing—I would so radiate that they will respect and revere mine as I respect theirs. When the Methodist says either in words or acts, "I am a Methodist and therefore you should be one," he violates the law of individuality as of moral freedom. So with the Hopi, the Catholic, the Hindoo.

I would have it clear, therefore, that individualism is not "toleration." What is there in my exercise of a God-given right and duty to be myself that should call for the assumption of my fellow being that HE will "tolerate" these rights? Therefore, I do not want to be "tolerant" to my fellows. I would radiate the individualism which goes ahead and thinks and acts according to the dictates of personal conscience. It is all very well to say that we should learn from the combined wisdom of the ages. I am not so sure of much of it, after all! I accept the astronomy of to-day, but by no means believe our astronomers have said the last word, any more than I believe that the great and humble Newton said the last word when he declared that man had gained the summit in the art of telescope making. Just four years after he made that foolish assertion John Dolland invented the achromatic telescope which has revolutionized the astronomical science of the world by adding infinitely to the astronomer's seeing power.

Nothing in human life is yet complete. There is *no* absolute truth carried out to its ultimate. When numbers were first discovered our forefathers thought they had gone as far as it was possible, in discovering that two and two make four. Then geometry was discovered and Euclid changed the arithmetic of the world, and the teachers said we had gone as far as it was possible. Then algebra was discovered and the world found out the teachers were wrong in limiting the science of arithmetic. Yet foolish people would not learn from the folly of the past. They wisely and sagely declared that *now, at last*, the ultimate had been reached. But Newton comes along and with his "Calculus" opens up new worlds in arithmetical science. NOW we have got it all, declares the teacher of *fixed* truth. Yet in the year of Our Lord, one thousand nineteen hundred and six, there comes a Japanese, and in his *Handbook of Chess* demonstrates as great an advance in arithmetical science as Newton did in his Calculus. We are yet children. We shall ever be learning so long as we are human. The knowledge we have so far gained is vast, apparently, when compared with the knowledge held in the Dark Ages, but, as compared *with what there is yet stored away for us to know*, I verily believe it is so insignificant, so slight, so small, so puny, so infinitesimal, as to excite the pity and the contempt of any superior beings who look down upon us and see us strutting in our doctor's mortar-boards and gowns in our assumed wisdom.

God forbid that any arrogant pretension of mine should ever prevent one truth from entering a human soul. I want to radiate my acceptance of all there is, but my expectance for the large *more* that is yet to come.

CHAPTER VI

CONFLICTING RADIANCIES

There are few, if any, human beings in the world who radiate only evil, or, on the other hand, only good. Man is a *human* being, not divine. Humanity implies a lower stage than divinity, and whether what we call evil be but manifestations of the imperfect and incomplete, or deliberate wrong choice for which one is personally responsible, we are all compelled to admit that there are few people with whom we meet who radiate toward us and all others only that which is good. Sometimes these "not good" radiancies have no immoral intent in them, though they produce bad results.

For instance, it is a well-known fact that many a man is driven to drunkenness by an unhappy home life, yet probably no member of the household has the deliberate intention of producing such a result. It may be that he is equally to blame for the conditions in his home, for all are imperfect, yet if the appetite for drink has been formed, or environment supplies great temptation, the complaints, taunts, or anger of his unhappy family do not increase his powers of resistance, but rather weaken them. There are men, also, who frankly confess to a reckless impulse to do wrong whenever they come under any very depressing influence. It may be true that some peculiarity of temperament renders them liable to be thrown out of mental balance. There may be inherent weakness, or hereditary tendency, which renders them unusually susceptible to depressing radiancies, but the results are just as deplorable.

Doubtless many a woman, too, warped and twisted out of normal conditions by disappointment, ill-treatment, and mental suffering, becomes a tongue-lasher, goes to the bad, or commits suicide, when different influences and environment would have saved her from such consequences. There may not seem to be any immorality in the nagging of a husband, or a wife, or a parent, yet the persistent nagging of some person, whose intent was only good, has produced direful effects in various ways.

These and a thousand other tendencies of the human being point to our present imperfection or subjugation to error, out of which we must rise.

I know a poet. His words have thrilled millions to a nobler and better life. His pen has never incited to a mean or ignoble thought or action; it has always written high and noble truth—peace, good will to men, the dignity of labor, the joy of helping, the blessing of purity, the never-failing help of God—and yet in his personal life he sometimes radiates the degradation of drunkenness and the awfulness of impurity.

I know a writer. He is one of the most brilliant men of his State. His knowledge is profound. He devotes more time, unselfishly, to the good of his adopted city and State than any other man I know. His work is untiring in its fervid zeal for the preservation of historic landmarks that without his efforts would possibly have disappeared; and also for a museum for the accumulation of evidences of past civilization. Yet he radiates a vindictive jealousy and fierce hatred of those whom he does not like that makes even his friends afraid of him and fearful lest they incur his anger.

Shelley, Byron, Poe, Bret Harte, Leigh Hunt, Landor—and thousands of others, including the Psalmist David, the Hebrew king whom God loved—radiated grand, sublime, divine truths, yet they also radiated weakness and moral wrong.

What should be our mental attitude toward those who give such conflicting radiancies? Shall we ignore the evil and see only the good? How *can* we? How *dare* we?

Shall we ignore the good and see only the evil?

Again I ask, How can we? How dare we?

There are good people, I know, who do both of these, to me, impossible things. I want to do neither. I will do neither if I can possibly help it. I will not stultify *my own* sense of right and wrong by ignoring what I deem to be wrong in another. I will reprobate it, for myself, and earnestly strive to be kept free from it, but, at the same time, I will see the good in all its beauty and power and will glorify it and accept it, and thank God that so much good does exist.

The whole question thus resolves itself to me: Shall I refuse to accept the good of certain men because they do many evil things? Shall I refuse to accept good except from those who are perfect? If so, from whom shall I gain good? From you, reader? Are you perfect? If you take that position you had better drop this book, here and now, for you cannot receive good from me, for too sadly do I know that neither the book nor its writer is perfect. Joaquin Miller perfectly expresses this thought in the introductory lines to his poem on Byron:

> In men whom men condemn as ill,
> I find so much of goodness still,
> In men whom men account divine,
> I find so much of sin and blot,
> I hesitate to draw the line between the two,
> Where God has not!

Let us be fearless, honest, just, frank. Too often we condemn people who have as much good as evil in them—or more—because we are afraid if we do not condemn the evil that they do, openly and loudly, people will think we tolerate evil because we ourselves are evil. Hawthorne wrote his *Scarlet Letter* to teach us different. The harsh, stern, vindictively pure and good people—in my humble judgment—have many and grave sins to answer for as well as those whom they so mercilessly condemn. I condemn all that which appears evil to me, and I seek to avoid it, but I condemn no man, no woman. That is not my privilege, my work. Judgment belongs to God who knows all circumstances and understands all hearts. I know and understand very little, for I am very short-sighted and ignorant. How can any of us look with so severe an eye upon the sins of our brothers and sisters when we, too, are imperfect, ignorant, prone to wrong. John Wesley taught the people of his denomination very differently, though they haven't yet learned the lesson. One of his hymns says:

> To hate sin with all my heart
> And yet the sinner love.

And the Lord of the whole Christian Church spoke in no uncertain terms when He said, "Judge Not," and in His action to those who brought the adulterous woman to Him clearly showed us what our attitude should be. Joaquin Miller wrote a much-needed lesson for this age, this civilization, this people (the puritanic American and Anglo-Saxon), when he took this incident in Christ's life and made it the theme of his poem, *Charity*. May its high and sympathetic truths sink deep, so that henceforth you will be able to stand side by side with the Divine in dealing with sinful men and women, and while condemning the sin be able to say: "Go, and sin no more." And, remember, it is not for you to say which sin is most sinful in God's sight. You may know which is of greater horror to yourself, but it may be that the "darling sin" you cherish in secret, or the "weakness" of your life may be regarded by the Divine as of great culpability as well as the "horrible sin" you so much deplore and feel you must condemn so bitterly in another.

CHAPTER VII

RADIANCIES OF FEAR

Fear is the greatest enemy of mankind. It is the creator of evil, for many people sin through fear. It is the maker of cowards and moral weaklings, the foe of all progress, the barrier to advancement, physical, mental, spiritual. He who is afraid dares not, and he who dares not, knows not, feels not, enjoys not. The fearful do not live; they merely exist, in bondage to a terror that leaves them neither night nor day. They know few of the delights of achievement, for they are afraid to dare. Fear throttles endeavor, stifles hope, murders aspiration. It is a hydra-headed monster of protean forms. It is a liar and a coward, a beguiler and a thief, a sneak and a poltroon, a slanderer and a cur. It comes in a thousand guises—sometimes as caution, then as tact, again as consideration for others, but ever and always as a deceiver and a destroyer.

If there is one thing above another that I wish I had learned in earliest youth, and I wish I had known enough to teach my children in their earliest days, it is perfect fearlessness. The only thing I fear to-day is fear. To go through life afraid of this and that and the other, is to take away all joy, all spontaneity, all freedom, all aspiration, all endeavor.

I used to believe and teach that we should "fear God." But the word "fear" as here used is not the abject, groveling, contemptible feeling that so many people imagine it to be. God has made us in His own image. He wishes us to stand upright, and greet Him as filial beings should, proud and glad to come to Him as "Our Father."

Fear makes us whine and whimper before God, and go to Him in the same spirit of dread that leads the Indian to feel he must always be propitiating the powers that be. If he does not pray and sing and dance and smoke the good powers will be offended, and will injure him, and the evil powers will be made more evil and do him more harm than they otherwise would. Hence month in and month out, because of fear, he seeks by his dances, and smokings, and songs, and prayers to protect himself from evil by soothing their possible anger and quieting their fury against him.

There is much of this same spirit in our old-time theology, and our present-day life. We are afraid of God. God doesn't want us to be afraid. Every man should therefore stand upright, afraid of neither God, man, nor devil. God is no tyrant to be turned from His purposes by sycophantic worship, or by "much speaking" and importunity. He is a reasonable God, a loving God, a just God, a merciful God, and abject fear will never change His plans as to His treatment of any human being.

As to being afraid of men, why should one man ever be afraid of another? Let us stand upright as men—one man just as good as another—*if he is as good,* and if he isn't as good, knowing that all the potentialities of godhead are within his own soul. We are gods, says Browning, though but as yet in the germ. Let us fearlessly develop the germ, or give it opportunity for development.

And as to being afraid of the devil, I have long since learned that the proper way to deal with what I suppose to be the devil—or his henchmen—is simply to straighten up my back, look him squarely in the eye, and definitely and positively bid him "Go to hell!" Even the most modest and refined of preachers, whether of the new or old type, will agree that that is the only place for the devil and his myrmidons.

I would have my children, myself, and the world afraid of nothing but of evil—and by evil I mean those sins that I myself know are evil—selfishness, pride, uncleanness, as well as the sins of the decalogue. But even here I would not let it be a fear that dreads falling into these sins. I would not anticipate or expect anything of the kind. Hence, in one sense I would not have them afraid of evil. Resist evil and it will flee from you. Harbor it not, do not dread it, but resolve to slay it by its opposite good. The evil is null if you live its opposite. There is no need for an unselfish man to fear selfishness. A man who gives freely never need fear that he will become a miser.

Yet people go through life afraid, and teach their children to be afraid, and thus lose nine-tenths of the love and joy and power and blessing of life.

Fear holds a large and powerful grip upon the human race. Scarce one woman in a thousand of the so-called civilized portion but is afraid of child-birth—a perfectly natural process that should be attended with all the angels of Love and Joy and Welcome, instead of the horrible demons of Fear.

From the time of birth until its body falls into the grave the mortal is taught fear. We pay preachers, teachers, lawyers, and doctors, and much of their work consists of fostering our fears. I have a picture before my mind's eye now of one of the noblest and best women that ever lived. Her whole life was a self-sacrifice, an unselfish devotion to others, yet, such was the theology that had been taught to her that she was constantly in dread lest she had done wrong, she was ever sitting on the stool of repentance, and life was a gloomy, somber, awful thing to her, because of her "dread of an angry God."

Thousands of people fear death because they have been taught that when they die they may "go to hell" for sins done on earth.

A mother was telling me only a few days ago of the perfect fearlessness of her boy until (when about six years of age) he went to a Sunday school, where they taught him their ideas of the devil and hell and God's method of punishing sin. That night he dared not go to bed without a light and woke up several times crying that he was afraid of sinking into hell.

Whatever preachers may feel it to be their duty to teach of hell and God's anger to grown men and women, I deem it monstrously cruel to put such fears into the plastic and trustful souls of the young.

Teachers, lawyers, and doctors are as bad as the preachers. We must avoid "night air," and draughts, and getting our feet wet, and not eating enough, and eating too much. We must not eat this and that, and must not do that or the other. Fear is instilled into our minds all along the pathway of life until if we are not healthy enough to throw it away and live our own fearless life, we are weighted down by the burden of our needless and senseless fears. All quack doctors work on the foolish and ignorant fears of the people, or their nostrums would never sell enough to pay a thousandth part of what their advertising costs. Fear is the club that scoundrels use to beat the ignorant into paying tribute to them.

I do not believe in these fears—to me they are all bad, and nothing but bad. I would banish every one of them from the human heart.

But, says an objector, you surely would not let your child go and handle a deadly rattlesnake, or send your growing and innocent girl into the company of expert *roués*, or willfully sleep in a miasmic atmosphere, or inhale the poisonous gases of a badly cared-for plumbing system? Of course not. But neither would I be afraid of them. There is all the difference in the world between *knowledge of danger*, and *fear* of that danger. Let a child be taught definitely and positively the danger of handling a rattlesnake, but do not fill his soul with fear of it; impress forcefully and strongly the wisdom of avoiding evil company upon your daughter, but teach her to be absolutely fearless in the presence of the debauchee; seek to the full how to avoid all miasma and deadly plumbing, but be fearless about them. Fear is the product of ignorance; fearlessness of knowledge. If my child knows all the harm a rattlesnake can do, and all the power it possesses, he can avoid it as easily as not. Therefore why should he be afraid? The feminine fears of mice, rats, spiders, and snakes are evidences either of ignorance, or of a developed hereditary tendency to fear. In the former case the fearful one should be trained so as to remove her fear, in the latter she should resolutely set her will to work to overcome it, in which all her friends should sympathetically aid her.

Fear has ever been the foe of progress. Every advance step in all life has been taken by him only who had throttled his fears. Fire was conquered for the human race by the man who dared brave the strange and weird flames that grew and then disappeared. Prometheus—the fearless—is the type of all who have helped the race to progress. It is the same in every field of endeavor, on every plane of thought. Galileo, Newton, Savonarola, the barons of King John's time, Cromwell, Luther, Bacon, Captain Cook, Washington, Lincoln are but a few of the thousands of names of men who have dared, who have bid their fears depart, and in so doing have advanced the human race.

Joaquin Miller in his grand poem *Columbus* clearly shows what would have become of him and the discovery of the new world had he let the fears of the mate and his sailors affect him. Read it carefully with this thought in view. Indeed it is well worth memorizing as a standing lesson against fear.

COLUMBUS

>Behind him lay the gray Azores,
>   Behind the Gates of Hercules;
>Before him not the ghost of shores;
>   Before him only shoreless seas.

The good mate said: "Now must we pray,
   For lo! the very stars are gone.
Brave Admir'l, speak; what shall I say?"
   "Why, say: 'Sail on! sail on! and on!'"

"My men grow mutinous day by day;
   My men grow ghastly wan and weak."
The stout mate thought of home; a spray
   Of salt wave washed his swarthy cheek.
"What shall I say, brave Admir'l, say,
   If we sight naught but seas at dawn?"
"Why, you shall say at break of day:
   'Sail on! sail on! sail on! and on!'"

They sailed and sailed, as winds might blow,
   Until at last the blanched mate said:
"Why, now, not even God would know
   Should I and all my men fall dead.
These very winds forget their way,
   For God from these dread seas is gone.
Now speak, brave Admir'l; speak and say———"
   He said: "Sail on! sail on! and on!"

They sailed. They sailed. Then spake the mate:
   "This mad sea shows his teeth to-night.
He curls his lip, he lies in wait,
   With lifted teeth, as if to bite!
Brave Admir'l, say but one good word:
   What shall we do when hope is gone?"
The words leapt like a leaping sword:
   "Sail on! sail on! sail on! and on!"

Then, pale and worn, he kept his deck,
   And peered through darkness. Ah, that night
Of all dark nights! and then a speck—
   A light! A light? A light! A light!
It grew, a starlit flag unfurled!
   It grew to be Time's burst of dawn.

> He gained a world; he gave that world
>   Its grandest lesson: "On! sail on!"[C]

Sydney Smith once well said: "A great deal of talent is lost to the world for want of a little courage. Every day sends to their graves men who have remained obscure because of timidity. The fact is that, in order to do anything in this world worth doing, we must not stand shivering on the brink and thinking of the cold and danger; but jump in and scramble through as well as we can. It will not do to be perpetually calculating risks, and adjusting nice chances. It did very well before the flood, when a man could consult his friends upon an intended publication for a hundred and fifty years, and live to see its success for six or seven centuries afterward. But at present a man waits, and doubts, and hesitates, and consults his father, brother, cousin, friends, till one fine day he finds he is sixty-five years of age. There is so little time for our squeamishness that it is no bad rule to preach up the necessity of a little violence done to the feelings and of efforts made in defiance of strict and sober calculation."

Too often elderly friends, with the best of intentions, inculcate this fear into the hearts of the young. Never was there a greater mistake or *real* unkindness. It is nothing that the intent is good. One's intent may palliate any judgment rendered against the offender, but, the unfortunate result, the implanting of the fear, cannot so easily be forgiven. Oh that I could prevail upon older people to refrain from this terribly demoralizing habit of giving advice to the young that inculcates fear. Let me illustrate:

A young man is a clerk in an office. He sees an opening to which his heart and brain strongly impel him, but there is a little, perhaps a great deal, of risk connected with it. He goes for advice to his older friends. They, with their life-work practically finished, valuing their rest and content more than desiring to reënter the battle of life, naturally are wary about an uncertainty. "Why not leave well enough alone? Why run the risk? What will you do if this fails? You will have given up a certainty for an uncertainty," and so on.

Ah! worldly wise though it *seems*, it is the most injurious and harmful advice that the young could possibly receive. Where would progress and advancement be to-day if many had not totally disregarded such smug, self-contented, unheroic advice! Thank God, youth is the time for adventure, for striking out, for *making mistakes*, for learning, for testing, for "proving *all* things," and holding fast to that which is good. Old age has had its day. It has made its mistakes and profited by them. Let it keep its hands off the young. Let them have their opportunity.

Herbert Spencer tells of throwing up a good job as civil engineer in order to experiment with a matter that a fortnight proved to be utterly impossible. Yet fifty years later he thus reviewed this apparently self-injurious act: "Had there not been this seemingly foolish act, I should have passed a humdrum and not very prosperous life as a civil engineer. That which has since been done would never have been done."

In other words, the act that shook him out of the rut, the contented, common, mediocre path, compelled him to find a new path for himself, and this called upon all the resources of his great and, to him and others, unknown nature, and he developed into the transcendent genius, the profound philosopher, whose writings had greater influence, perhaps, upon his century than those of any other man.

Hence I want to radiate the spirit of complete fearlessness, not only for myself, but for my young friends of both sexes, all the sons and daughters of men. I would calmly watch them plunge overboard into the ocean of life, trustful and confident, having first taught them the first few strokes of swimming—the principles of true and godly living—and then stand, fearlessly, and watch them strike out for themselves. I swam,—why should not they? God is in His heaven to-day watching the sparrows fly just as He was a score, a hundred, a thousand years ago.

In the mental world how fearful people often are of breaking away from old ideas. Only the other day a friend wrote me that he had been to a funeral, conducted by an orthodox clergyman. He said: "I imagine his is a very orthodox denomination, if he is a fair sample of what they believe. Glimmerings of a soul that hungers for larger things than its creed allowed was evident in his talk, however. Is it not pitiful, and more, is it not tragical, how people allow their soul-instincts and natural outreachings to be killed, or hampered, or stilled by what their befuddled brains or the brains of others have decided is proper, or accepted as proper, to believe?"

I can remember when good Methodists and Congregationalists were "kicked out of the church" for daring to hope that all men would ultimately be saved, and I have heard preachers and doctors fulminating against

Christian Science and everything else that did not conform exactly to what they believed, and seeking to work upon the fears of their congregations to prevent any investigation. This kind of fear is unworthy the human soul. Be in a daring, a receptive, an investigative state of mind. I would radiate a readiness and willingness to listen to anything that has proven, or seems to have proven, a truth to another. I want to welcome truth from wherever it comes, whether popular or unpopular, wanted or unwanted. I would broaden my horizon, heighten my aspirations and deepen my conceptions of truth and be glad to receive from any source. I well remember John Ruskin saying to me: "Never read that book or listen to that sermon which you know beforehand you will agree with. By so doing you deepen the ruts of your own mentality." I want no mental or spiritual ruts. Good roads are never "rutted." I wish to be a broad, wide, well-paved, solid road, over which all truth may run, welcome, free, untaxed, life-giving.

In his *Memory and Rime,* Joaquin Miller in speaking of poets refers to them as "these men who have room and strength and the divine audacity to think for themselves."

When a man strikes out for himself, in thought and action, he does have to be audacious, in the higher sense of the word. He has to dare his fellow men, dare their criticism, dare their disapproval, dare to shock them, dare to grieve them, perhaps. He has to dare himself, throw down the gauntlet to himself in his struggle to become completely what he believes to be highest and best. It takes a great deal of courage to do all that, a great deal of resolution—an initiative that may seem impudence, a fearlessness that may seem recklessness.

The strength that makes it possible to do this must be a strength like to the divine strength. A strength ordained from the foundation of the earth as a part of man's birthright, to become a part of himself, when he begins to try for himself to conceive of higher good and to live it. The man who thinks only as other men think, dares act only as other men act, is as a babe in swaddling clothes, helpless, dependent. One can never be strong until he learns to walk alone, independent of another's hand to cling to or another's strength to steady himself by. One must learn to stand on his own feet, learn to keep his own balance, learn to step by his own volition. If he does not he becomes a cripple. Most lives are as the lives of cripples, and we help to make them so by our continued trying to force people to cling to us and our ideas, frightening them into believing that they are in great danger if they try to step alone. A little trembling of the legs as one first stands alone is nothing to be alarmed at. A few falls and bumps as we first step out never seriously injure us.

It is only when a life has strength to stand out alone, independent of its fellows, that its soul can take hold of God.

And I fancy that it is only when a life thinks and acts for itself, and allows its fellow men to think and act for themselves, that it is in a condition to really give help and to receive help, really in a state of mind to fulfill the commandment: "Thou shalt love thy neighbor as thyself."

It is one thing to be brave enough to do something which is hard to do but which your fellow men will approve of your doing, and an entirely different thing to do something hard but which your fellow men will not approve of your doing. Therefore I want to radiate into actual, living potentiality my belief that life consists in expression and not repression. By many this is taken to be a plea for license and want of self-control. Do not believe it! That is not what I mean. The expression of evil is not the expression of myself, for I long to do only good. Read what St. Paul says on the subject. And by "I," I mean my real self, as Paul did—not my lower self, my evil heredity, or whatever it is that seeks to drive away the good from me—I, the real I, the self which is, and which may not appear to the world, want to express all that is in that real self. That means that I must control, slay, kill, drive out all the evil that comes to me and demands that I express it as part of myself. It is not a part of my spiritual self, and if I express evil then I am not myself in that sense. But I want to have such perfect, such absolute control over all outward expressions that I shall ever and at all times express nothing but that which is good; and that which will be felt to be good by all people.

And yet we must determine what we should express. The thinking man and woman make their own standards. These standards, in certain great principles of honor, truth, nobleness, purity, are practically alike, yet most men and women are controlled by fashion, custom, society, rather than by their own cool, deliberate judgment. I want to radiate my protest against this state of affairs. I will be my own judge and not place the responsibility for my own moral life upon the judgment of any person, society, clique, class, or church. I must be saved by my own belief and life, not by the belief and life of others.

For years I endeavored to "avoid the appearance of evil." When at last, however, I discovered that the "appearance of evil"—the determination of what it was, rested upon the average quality of the minds of the community by which I was surrounded, and not always upon right, or truth, or justice, I made up my mind that for me, at least, God had a higher mission. I resolved, therefore, in His strength fearlessly to radiate a higher conception of things. An evil mind sees evil where none is; a filthy mind sees filth where is only innocence and sweetness. Was I to shape my life and conduct to meet the ideas of those who deem innocence and trustfulness, natural simplicity, and true-heartedness as "appearances of evil"? God forbid. Rather, by far, would I suffer in the judgments of men and women, cruel and untrue though they would be, than forego the life of natural trust, simple uprightness, that alone mean *life* to me.

And this is what I desire to radiate,—a positive, powerful, healthful, aseptic moral quality that will refuse to allow people to see evil where none exists; that will lead them to prefer to see, to hope for, to believe in, the good rather than the evil in men. Better trust and be deceived, than live a life of horrible mistrust. I know men and women are imperfect, and, like myself, composed of good and evil, therefore I am determined to radiate my belief in the good in them rather than radiate my belief in the bad of them.

It is worth while to re-read George Eliot's *Mill on the Floss*, to see how poor Maggie Tulliver was misjudged and cruelly treated purely on what people *supposed* was her wrong-doing. And I shall never forget the influence the following words had on me when I first read them. I would that the lesson they contain might be burned into the inmost consciousness of every reader of this book.

> Even on the supposition that required the utmost stretch of belief—namely, that none of the things said about Miss Tulliver were true—still, since they *had* been said about her, they had cast an odor around her which must cause her to be shrunk from by every woman who had to take care of her own reputation—and of society. To have taken Maggie by the hand and said, 'I will not believe unproved evil of you; my lips shall not utter it; my

ears shall be closed against it; I, too, am an erring mortal, liable to stumble, apt to come short of my most earnest efforts, your lot has been harder than mine, your temptation greater; let us help each other to stand and walk without more falling;'—to have done this would have demanded courage, deep pity, self-knowledge, generous trust—would have demanded a mind that tasted no piquancy in evil speaking, that felt no self-exaltation in condemning, that cheated itself with no large words into the belief that life can have any moral end, any high religion, which excludes the striving after perfect truth, justice, and love towards the individual men and women who come across our own path.

It is my earnest desire that I may radiate this spirit of courage, deep pity, self-knowledge, generous trust, and all that follows. And this, not in an abstract or theoretical way, but in the real concrete cases that one meets with in life. I am not too good to associate with the found-out wrong-doer if he is striving against his wrong-doing, and aiming to be better. I would not look down on any human being because of any sin. Though I want to grow to hate sin more and more as the manifestations of that which separates us from the Infinite, I want the sinner to feel that I am one with him in all desire to be free from evil, to be possessed only by the spirit of truth, purity, and love.

All great victories whether of peace or war have been won by the fearless, the unafraid. We honor the heroes of the past, of Thermopylæ, and the fearless and brave of all nations and all time. Tennyson's *Charge of the Light Brigade* appeals to our love and respect for the virile, the manly, the courageous, the fearless, and it is the same spirit that thrills us when we read or hear *Curfew Shall not Ring To-night*. To save her lover the shrinking maiden was filled with high born courage and dared to hang on to the bell. Whether we agree with his beliefs or not we admire the bravery of Luther that led him to exclaim: "Were there as many devils in my way as tiles on the house tops yet would I go to Worms." Whether we approve of his ascetic life or not we thrill at the bravery, the simple-hearted daring of Francis of Assisi, who resolutely cast aside his patrimony and dared his father's anger that he might serve God in his own way.

Every advanced thinker, whose life and action spell progress for the race, has to be a daring pioneer. He must be an iconoclast; he must be self-contained, self-assured, self-confident. He must stand aloof from his fellows in the very spirit of the message he brings, for he dares—imperfect, weak, even sinful though he be—to be a teacher, a leader of others. And how natural, human, it is for those who live with or near him, seeing and knowing as they do, all his foibles, weaknesses, littlenesses, failures, sins, to magnify these things and by them hide the beauty and grandeur of the lesson God has given him to teach the world.

Our poets have given us some wonderfully vivid pictures of the fearless. Perhaps the greatest in all literature is Shelley's *Prometheus*. It is worth reading a score of times in order that its spirit of fearlessness might be absorbed. Joaquin Miller's *Columbus*, which I have already quoted, gives a marvelously vivid picture of the great admiral when even hope had gone from his own heart, when he could not pierce by faith the darkness of his own soul.

> Then, pale and worn, he kept his deck,
> And peered through darkness. Ah, that night
> Of all dark nights!

Yet though it was all darkness *to* his own soul, and *in* his own soul, he kept on. His orders were "Sail on!" And his courage and bravery brought him to the light of the new world.

Browning in his *Prospice* opens with the bold and daring interrogative: "Fear death?" and, after showing what there is to fear, exclaims as in an ecstasy of fearlessness:

> I would hate that death bandaged my eyes, and forebore
> And bade me creep past.
> No! let me fare like my peers, the heroes of old.
> In a minute pay, glad, life's arrears
> Of pain, darkness, and cold.

I want to radiate the active consciousness even when I am storm-tossed, beaten down by fierce winds, compelled to stay my journey by the sand-laden, hot sirocco of the desert, dashed upon the cruel rocks by tempestuous waves, frozen by the blizzards of the North, that I have nothing to fear, that nothing can harm me save myself, that God is over all and in all. As David called upon mountains, and all hills, fire, and hail, snow and vapors, stormy wind, to praise Him, fulfilling His word, so would I call. And in calling I would rest and be at peace.

And I want to radiate to others my fearlessness for them. They need not fear though the heavens fall. Many a man fails in the fierce conflict raging in his own soul because he has been taught to fear the fierce judgment of an angry God. I want with all the vehemence of my nature to radiate a spirit that will kill and bury forever such fear in human souls. Let no one daunt you by such teaching. Under all circumstances, brother, keep your face up!

Look ever to the stars!

If, in the conflict, you lose heart, do not let your face down so as to be covered by the mud into which you are sinking. Battle on, though you are finally swallowed up—or fear you will be. Go down face up, and let the last thing your expiring gaze rests upon, be the stars above. Though the mud and mire cover your mouth so that you cannot cry out,

Look up to the stars!

Though it rise higher, and cover your nostrils so that you cease to breath,

Look up to the stars!

Though it flows into your very eyes,

Look up to the stars!

My word for it, my soul for yours, the God of men will take that last expiring glance of yours and make it the lever that shall pull you out of the mire and set your feet upon the rock and establish your goings, and

Put a new song into your mouth.

CHAPTER VIII

THE RADIANCY OF REBUKE

I want to radiate the ability to rebuke without offense, although this may appear to be a singular desire. One night I sat with a friend enjoying the exquisite music of the Boston Symphony Orchestra. During one of the most subtle and delicate passages a "lady" in the seat behind me began to whisper to her escort. It was as the thrusting of a bottle of sulphuretted hydrogen under my nose when I was enjoying the subtle essence of a violet.

Four times that evening did that "cultured" Boston savage outrage my susceptibilities by her rudeness, by her theft of my power and right of enjoyment.

I wanted to rebuke her, and I did not know how, without giving her offense. I used to offend such offenders and glory in my share of the offense. I hope I have learned better,—yet, all the same, I do wish to administer some rebuke, that will be effective. As I have said elsewhere, I want to do this so that my own serenity is preserved. Thus shall I radiate serenity and not offense. If I am disturbed, offended, outraged, I radiate those vibrations of unrest and disturbance. I would reprove kindly, but surely and effectively, and that is best done by bringing the offender into sympathy with the best that I desire for him as well as myself.

I would that I could rebuke every boy who keeps a seat in a car when an elderly or aged man or woman stands by unseated.

I would that I could rebuke every parent who fails to teach his or her child his duty in this regard.

I would that I could rebuke every parent who fails to require absolute and explicit obedience to authority—his own and all other proper authorities—on the part of his or her child.

I would that I could rebuke every irreverent person whether in Catholic Cathedral, Episcopal Church, Methodist Chapel, Congregational Meetinghouse, Navaho Hogan, Hopi Kiva, or Chinese Joss House, who laugh, sneer, talk aloud, or in other vulgar way show their irreverence. All are sacred to some one—all should alike be reverenced.

I would that I could rebuke every haughty purse-proud woman or man who *demands* service, not through love, but by power of money or fear.

And my rebuke list would include the politician who uses his office for graft, the senator who sells his vote, the legislator who hesitates to give his interest and vote to all bills that seek the true welfare of the common people. It would include every purveyor of adulterated foods for the people, every user of child labor, every employer of sweated labor, and every "bargain-counter" fiend who hunts for the product of the sweat-shop. It would include every newspaper owner who allows prejudice to control his columns rather than fairness, and makes himself a party to the willful deception of the people; every lawyer who values fees more than justice; every physician a case more than health; every preacher a fat salary more than truth.

And it might include you, reader, did I know you as well as I know myself, whom I rebuke constantly.

CHAPTER IX

WHAT I WOULD RADIATE TO THE WRONG DOER

For two years I was the chaplain for two homes where women who had led evil lives were sheltered and cared for. During part of this time I helped organize and conduct a midnight mission in one of the most degraded parts of a large eastern city. I have had a large and varied acquaintance with criminals of both sexes, of all ages and conditions, and have been the recipient of many strange and startling confidences of men and women whose integrity has never been questioned, and yet who, if their inner life were known, would have been execrated and ostracized.

As a result of these varied experiences and the knowledge that has come to me I am compelled to assert that I believe our present system of treatment of wrong-doers is not only unchristian but unwise and foolish, and that it fosters and cherishes some of the very wrongs we seek to prevent.

The attitude we take—that every evil doer loves his evil doing, sins because he wants to sin, is a criminal for his own pleasure—is absurd and foolish. And what wicked cruelties such an attitude leads us to commit. Socrates saw clearer than that centuries ago when he said: "It is strange that you should not be angry when you meet a man with an ill-conditioned body, and yet be vexed when you encounter one with an ill-conditioned soul!"

Most of us have a lot of maxims or rules that we apply to those wrong-doers who come under our ken, forgetful of the fact that the strange thing about human nature is that it doesn't fit your, or my, or any one's ideas or notions. It cannot be bounded, as you bound a sea or an island. It cannot be plotted or catalogued as you plot a lawn or catalogue a library. The only way you can read men and women is with sympathy and love—sympathy for their failures to measure up to your conceptions of manhood and womanhood; love for the undoubted good that you perceive.

All moral judgments must remain false and hollow that are not checked and enlightened by a perpetual reference to the special circumstances that mark the individual lot.

Christ did not in the least abrogate the Seventh Commandment when he said to the woman *taken in the act* of adultery: "I do not condemn thee. Go and sin no more." In my opinion He wished to teach the lesson that the self-righteousness and hypocrisy of her accusers were also crimes.

All men that are drunkards are not equally culpable, deserving of hell-fire and to be swept there by quoting the Hebrew scriptures: "No drunkard shall inherit eternal life." The special circumstances must be considered, and God only is competent to do this. Whenever I hear these ready quotations, whenever I am tempted to use them in my dealings with my erring fellow-men and women I recall what George Eliot wrote in *The Mill on the Floss*.

> All people of broad, strong sense have an instinctive repugnance to the men of maxims; because such people early discern that the mysterious complexity of our life is not to be embraced by maxims, and that to lace ourselves up in formulas of that sort is to repress all the divine promptings and inspirations that spring from growing insight and sympathy. And the man of maxims is the popular representative of the minds that are guided in their moral judgment safely by general rules, thinking that these will lead them to justice by a ready-made patent method, without the trouble of exerting patience, discrimination, impartiality,— without any care to assure themselves whether they have the insight that comes from a hardly earned estimate of temptation, or from a life vivid and intense enough to have created a wide fellow-feeling with all that is human.

The true brotherhood of man is that which takes upon itself all the weaknesses, all the burdens, all the woes, all the sins of the world of men and women. This is what Christ did! Ah, that we might perceive and realize it! This is what makes Walt Whitman so great a poet,—that he tries to teach us this lesson. This is what gave to Ernest Crosby his power, gave to Golden Rule Jones his influence. They felt the brotherhood, truly, really, deeply, even though imperfectly. Christ felt it perfectly. Can we not try to feel it? Whenever we behold sin in others it behooves us to remember that Paul said, "*All* have sinned and come short of the glory of God," and that whenever we condemn sin in another we condemn some sin in ourselves. We are all sinners in some way or another. There are those who feel the oneness of human relationship so keenly that they have declared that when another did a wrong they felt it as if it were their own personal act. While I have not yet come to so close a recognition of my brotherhood to all men and women as that, I can deeply sympathize with the feeling. We all know how a brother feels if one of his own family—sister or brother—"goes wrong." He is grieved and disgraced. A burden is placed upon him. When we fully recognize the brotherhood we owe to all men and women I doubt not we shall then feel this personal sorrow and disgrace, which will lead us to seek our brother's speedy reclamation, with helpful sympathy and loving encouragement.

Only those touched with the essential spirit of the love that belongs to the Divine, or those who have sinned much, can know the great secret of human tenderness and long suffering towards the wrong doer that alone, *at times*, can help him. Oh for more of this human tenderness and sympathy, this long suffering and patience, this active principle of Divine Love that burns through all crusts and coatings of evil into the most secret corners of the heart where the good is enshrined, though forgotten.

I have just been talking with a prominent editor about a man in his office, competent, thorough, reliable, manly, a systematic worker and able to get the best results out of those in his department, yet who, once in a while, goes off on a terrible debauch. He will drink up all the money at hand, then draw out whatever he has saved in the bank (sometimes nearly a thousand dollars), engage an automobile, surround himself with dissolute companions, squander his money on them, then borrow from his friends, who, knowing that when sober he will pay back every cent, cruelly lend it to him, and thus "go the pace" until either money gives out, or physical endurance can no longer stand the strain. Then his true friends come and pick him up out of the gutter, or care for him in a hospital until he recovers.

As soon as he is sane and sober again he is overwhelmed with remorse and sorrow. He knows that he is ruining himself in every way and from every possible standpoint, yet there is that in him that seems to render him incapable of resisting these temptations to periodical sprees. He listens with true penitence to the cautions of his employers, his fellow workers, and to the heart-broken pleadings of his aged mother who fairly idolizes him—still he drinks.

What shall I radiate to such a man—to all such men? Can I ignore the degradation of their debauchery? Certainly not! Can I ignore the fact that, as a rule, when the downward path is once begun, the sober intervals grow shorter after each debauch, and that by radiating friendliness to such a man I am tying myself to one who will ultimately disgrace himself and me? Shall I cease to be his friend, in order to protect myself?

God forbid! To radiate friendliness is not enough. Seek to possess more than this, that you may radiate more. Greater than friendship is love. Love your friend as yourself. He is having a desperate struggle. Give him your love, your thoughtful, considerate, protective love. If necessary treat him as you would an insane person, for the highest medical experts now concede that "while alcoholic excess is a prolific source of disease and mental instability, *disease and mental instability are even more provocative of the alcoholic habit.*" The greatest possible kindness to such an one would be to lovingly, tenderly, sympathetically *lock him up*. The insane man must be kept from doing himself and others an injury. Society must protect itself from the evil doer, regardless of his moral responsibility, but the "how" of that protection is one of the most important things in the development of the human race. As we now protect ourselves we show the barbarity of the aborigine, the cruel vindictiveness of the savage.

I am fully satisfied that the time will come when we shall so radiate Christian love one to another, and especially to our weaker brothers and sisters—whether their weaknesses manifest themselves in alcoholic excess, sexual sins, gambling, theft, drug-manias, or any other form of wrong-doing—that we shall prepare for them places where they may be properly cared for, and especially whenever they fear they are in danger of succumbing to their weaknesses. This method would not apply to those who are so enthralled by sin that they think they find great pleasure in the gross gratification of the senses, for such are doomed to suffer until they are forced to see their errors and turn from them with loathing, but there are others who are unwilling victims to appetite and evil habits. The burdens which weak humanity carries are many and complex, and sometimes even mysterious. It is known to the medical world that many wrong deeds and even serious crimes are committed by men and women under temporary abnormal mental conditions. In Scriptural times doubtless it would have been said that they were possessed with demons, but the modern expert calls such conditions *manias* of various kinds. Whatever the subtle cause of this species of insanity, it is generally admitted that the attacks are of a periodical nature, and that during the intervals the victims conduct themselves in accordance with ordinary standards. Condemnation and ostracism cannot remedy such evils, but true Christianity should prompt a method of treatment that will encourage and sustain rather than induce despair. Even ordinary so-called "sinners" are not reclaimed by avoiding them utterly. Those who go down into the slums and plague-spots of our cities would never rescue any of the "perishing" if they went grudgingly, and holding themselves daintily aloof in self-righteous superiority. No, they brave the pestilential radiation in perfect safety and carry hope to the fallen because they possess the mind of Christ, which is purity and love. This does not alter the fact that the pure and good naturally shrink from depravity and degradation, nor that it is expedient to protect the ignorant and innocent from association with those who radiate impurity, oftentimes, but since it is well known that society contains many men and some women whose private lives would not stand publicity, the only safeguard is to be fortified within with that purity and goodness which involuntarily resists evil and imparts good.

CHAPTER X

THE RADIANCIES OF TOLERATION

I want to radiate my conception of what, in religion, is commonly termed "toleration." To me the term is a misnomer. Its use is based upon a gross and small-minded misunderstanding of the right, inherent to each human being, to live according to the dictates of his own conscience in all things that do not militate against what the majority conceive to be the public good.

What is religion? My own definition is that *it is the highest within myself reaching out to the highest I can see or conceive outside of myself.* In this "reaching out," this "following after," or "apprehending," as St. Paul calls it, I alone must determine that which I will seek for. Others may aid me in my search, others may point out to me and for me that which they have reached, or are striving to reach, and in that way they may aid and help me. But for another to say, "*This* is that alone for which you should strive," or "That is the supreme end of all effort," and to refuse me any right of appeal to my own judgment is to stultify my own God-given powers and to make a mere puppet of me. Hence I stand, or fall, on the platform of individualism in religion. I affirm that it is a purely personal matter, that there can be no coercion, no forcing of any individual to adopt a *general* plan which another individual asserts that all must follow to their eternal well-being, or disregard to their own damnation.

The attitude I would radiate is this. For myself I know, or am learning, what I must believe, what I must strive for, what I must seek to become. So long as this belief, this striving, this aim, does not interfere with the exercise of the belief, the striving, the aim of others, and is not subversive of the public good, I demand my inherent right of individual belief, individual striving, individual aim. When one who differs from me offers me his "charity," or his "toleration," I regard his offer as an insolence and small-minded impertinence. I want no charity, I refuse all toleration, for I own as many inherent rights as the one who thus presumes to offer me his charity and his tolerance. He needs my charity and tolerance to cover his individualism as much as I need his. I have as much right to offer mine to him as he to offer his to me. Hence, boldly, fearlessly, restful in my God-given right, I believe, I strive, I aim to reach God as best I may. But in the very self-assertiveness of this right it is an essential condition of my perfect freedom that I absolutely accord it to all others, no matter how diverse from mine their beliefs, their strivings, their aims. There must be no mental reservations, no subterfuges, no playing with one's own intellect or conscience. The freedom to others must be as large and complete as the freedom I demand for myself, for, wherein I limit, even in my most secret mind and heart, the freedom of my neighbor, I am giving to him the right to limit me. "With what measure ye mete it shall be measured to you again."

I resent any interference with my right to believe as I choose. My friends, G—— and S——, are Catholics. In the exercise of their God-given right they accept a different faith from mine. They are equally earnest, equally intelligent, equally sincere in their profession of faith as am I. Just as I resent any interference with my own right to believe as I choose, so do I resent, with equal, and even stronger fervor, any interference with G——'s and S——'s rights to believe as they choose.

I say with "even stronger fervor." You may ask, "Why with stronger fervor?" The reason is this. I find, within my own soul, a greater readiness to demand freedom for myself than I do to accord it to those who differ from me. Hence honor demands that I watch with even closer scrutiny the rights of my neighbors than I guard against encroachments upon my own. Selfishness will care for my own. Indifference to my neighbors *may* lead me to be careless of theirs.

Other neighbors, P—— and X——, are Christian Scientists; still others, A—— and J——, are Unitarians; others, D—— and C——, are Universalists; and I have friends, dear to my heart, whom I love with true, pure fervor and who, I am assured, love me with an equal sincerity, who are Jews, Hopis, Wallapais, Havasupais, Apaches, Greeks, Mohammedans, Hindoos, Theosophists, Spiritualists, Atheists, Shakers, Agnostics, Communists, and Mormons. Take these beliefs and non-beliefs with the one I profess and the others I have referred to, and there is as perfect a hodge-podge of diversities and differences as one can possibly imagine. Do I attempt to reconcile them? No! Do I agree with them all? No! Can I harmonize them all? No! It is neither my business to reconcile them, agree with them, nor harmonize them. I am not sent to earth to make all men's minds and souls alike, any more than Burbank is sent to make all flowers and plants, shrubs and trees alike. My business is to develop and live my own life, in harmony with my own beliefs, aims, and strivings, to the utmost, and seek the utmost good for my fellow. And in no way can I better do that than by aiding him to live his highest beliefs to the utmost, helping him in his strivings, make clearer to him the beauty of his own aims. Hence, even as I want all good men and true to bid me a hearty, an earnest, a sincere "God-speed!" in my own strivings, so do I, with all my heart, bid my many and diverse-believing, diverse-aiming friends God-speed in their endeavors.

If, for the public good, I should ever be called upon to pass judgment upon any of the actions that are the result of the beliefs of my neighbors and friends, and I, with my fellow jurors, deemed these actions subversive of the public good, I could unite with my fellows in suppressing these actions. But this would be done with a perfectly open heart, without malice, without censure even, without any presumption, without any interference with the *principle* I have sought clearly to state and exemplify. It would be done as the result of our united judgment upon a matter of public policy—not a fixed, established assurance of right or wrong, but as a matter wherein, for the benefit of others, we regarded the restriction of an inherent and God-given freedom a justifiable act.

Herein, to my mind, lies the power of the argument of the political prohibitionists. They seek to prohibit men from the exercise of their undoubted right to manufacture and sell alcoholic stimulants—their undoubted right provided it could be done without injury to the bodies and souls of their fellow-beings. No one can claim an inherent right to injure his neighbor willfully and deliberately. No one can claim a God-given right to transgress God's own laws. Those who believe in God believe He has ordained laws for the government of all that He has created. The interpretation of the "moral law" as handed down to us in the Scriptures is, in the main, similar in all creeds in Christendom, and practically the same among all who, without so-called creeds, believe in the brotherhood of man.

Upon those points wherein men have conscientiously differed there have been instances where the ruling majority has restricted or taken away the rights of the minority to put their beliefs into practice, because the consensus of opinion has decided such acts to be contrary to public policy or public good, but it does not necessarily follow that the interference was based upon incontrovertible ideas of right or wrong.

My contention is that no man or body of men has the inherent right to interfere with the beliefs and acts of their fellow-beings who are sincerely and conscientiously seeking to love God with all the heart and their neighbors as themselves, but in all countries where the majority is supposed to rule it is expedient to submit to prevailing customs and laws unless conscience imperatively demands otherwise. In any case, however, it does not necessarily follow that the majority is always in the right and the minority in the wrong, especially in religious matters.

CHAPTER XI

OUT OF DOOR RADIANCIES

I want to radiate a constant, never-failing love for God's great out of doors at all times, in all seasons, under all conditions, in all moods. I want to understand Nature, to be one with her, to feel with her, expand with her, be reserved with her, be exuberant with her. I want to realize and radiate my kinship with everything that exists in Nature; I am a part of this great whole, all of which is an expression of a great thought of the great God. By making myself a part of Nature I am able to make allies of all the forces of Nature, and this fact I want to radiate with power and emphasis. I would teach both by word, influence, and unconscious radiation that we are able to ally ourselves with all the powers of God as manifested in the world around us. I have learned that, no matter for whom else the sun may shine, it shines expressly for me. I would have you learn that it shines expressly for you. Whatever its power it belongs to you. Claim it! And so with all the forces. The winds blow for you, the flowers bloom for you, the stars glisten for you, the fruits grow for you, the trees clothe themselves in beauty for you, the birds sing for you, the sunsets are glorious for you, and the sunrises gild the mountain tops with reddish gold for you, the grass grows for you, the creeks sing, the rivers flow, and the seas roar for you; the forces of good are all yours, you are allies with them, and what they are you are, what power they possess, you possess.

What marvelous vivification comes into the body, mind, and soul of man when he realizes this stupendous fact. He no longer stands alone on the earth. God, to many men and women, is far away, unseen, unknowable, but through His world in Nature we can touch Him, realize Him, learn to know Him, and while we are learning this greatest of great facts we are becoming stronger, more self-reliant, more full of power, more optimistic, more sure of our own footing on earth.

A man may not say of a palace, a house, a garden, a yacht, a fortune, this, these, are mine, but we may each and all—the vilest drunkard, the most wretched harlot, the near-suicide, and the nigh-insane, as well as the poverty-stricken and the oppressed—say and know "the sun is mine, the stars, the rain, the sweetness of the flowers, the blessedness of God's great gift of life. Therefore, I am not poor, I am not forsaken, I am not forgotten. I own much. I will take and utilize these for my eternal blessing."

And as you utilize what you have you become both capable and worthy of larger things. Only those who use receive more. "To him that hath shall be given," and these are the things that all may have and that bless more abundantly than any other things mankind may possess.

Most of us go through life missing what Nature has for us.

In one of Sienkiewicz's books he makes one of his characters say of his betrothed,

> I gaze on Nature, too, and feel it; but she shows me things which I should not notice myself. A couple of days ago, we all went into the forest, where she showed me ferns in the sun, for instance. They are so delicate! She taught me also that the trunks of pine-trees, especially in the evening light, have a violet tone. She opens my eyes to colors which I have not seen hitherto, and, like a kind of enchantress going through the forest, discloses new worlds to me.

Reread these two sentences: "She shows me things which I should not notice myself," and "She opens my eyes and discloses new worlds to me." The world's beauty is so common to us that we forget it. Nothing is commoner than the stars, yet nothing more mysterious, wonderful, and attractive; the grass is so common that we trample it under foot, yet its beauty, its varied features will repay long hours of study, and it is a joy unspeakable to those who have learned to love it. It is in the common things that we should look for beauty, for lessons in color, in art, in criticism. One of the great students and teachers of art of our country once wrote a book entitled *The Gate Beautiful*. It was the result of a life of concentrated study upon true art. Whence comes true art? What is it? How shall one know it when he sees it? The result of all Dr. Stimson's study, placed in that wonderful book, summed up in short is—study Nature, and you will there learn more than all the books and teachers of art can tell you in a thousand years. The author shows by remarkable illustrations spiral vibrations made by the voice, the natural forms of mineralogy, mechanics, astronomy, seeds, fruit, vegetables, fish, reptiles, insects, birds, beasts, flowers, and humanity.

He shows the exquisite beauty of snow crystals, and of the minute forms of earliest life, found in the diatoms. He sets forth the beauty of leaf and stem in the commonest trees, in shells, etc., until one wonders where his eyes have been, where his appreciation of beauty, in all the years that these things have not appealed to him. Nature is so flooded with beauty that more than one lifetime will be necessary for any one man to discover the half of it. So because of its beauty I want the men and women who come in contact with me to feel in me a pulsing, living, active, irresistible love for Nature which will draw them out into it; arouse in them an insatiable longing to see and know, to feel and comprehend more of the rich beauty so freely exposed out of doors.

The out-of-doors, too, is full of beauty of color as well as beauty in form. Oh, the sunrises and sunsets at sea, and on the desert, and in the canyons, and on the mountain heights, and on the great plains of Arizona and New Mexico and Utah. What colorist of earth can ever equal them? Titian? Tintoretto? Velasquez? Turner? La Farge? Reid? Why waste words asking the questions? How tame is Titian's greatest color-effects side by side with a sunrise on the ocean, or a sunset on the desert! Bostonians are proud of Reid's magnificent paintings in the State House. I enjoy them myself and do not wonder that visitors are struck by the powerful color-handling of the interesting historical subjects. But Mr. Reid himself is not so foolish as to imagine that his greatest paintings are more than futile attempts to put on canvas the colors his eyes have seen, his soul has felt, out in the open. So, for color I would radiate a love for out-of-doors.

And I would radiate a love for all of out-of-doors at all times. Winter, Summer, Spring, Autumn, in rain and sunshine, in storm and calm, there is something in every condition, every mood for the men and women who are receptive. When I see newly born infants shut out from the pure air, their faces covered, "lest they take cold," I am filled with amazement at people's fear of out-of-doors. My babies were put to sleep out-of-doors half an hour after they were born. The latest and most approved methods of treating tuberculosis is to make those afflicted with it sleep out of doors. There are camps in Michigan and in the snowy regions of New York, in the Adirondacks, where, throughout the Winter, patients sleep out of doors with the best of results. Be not afraid. Go out of doors as does the Indian. Learn of him and be wise. He is a believer in the virtue of the outdoor life, not as an occasional thing, but as his regular, uniform habit. He *lives* out of doors; and not only does his body remain in the open, but his mind, his soul, are ever also there. Except in the very cold weather his house is free to every breeze that blows. He laughs at "drafts." "Catching cold" is something of which he knows absolutely nothing. When he learns of white people shutting themselves up in houses into which the fresh, pure, free air of the plains and deserts, often laden with the healthful odors of the pines, firs, and balsams of the forest, cannot come, he shakes his head at the folly, and feels as one would if he saw a man slamming his door in the face of his best friend. Virtually he sleeps out of doors, eats out of doors, works out of doors. When the women make their baskets and pottery, it is always out of doors, and their best beadwork is always done in the open. The men make their bows and arrows, dress their buckskin, make their moccasins and buckskin clothes, and perform nearly all their ceremonials out-of-doors.

I wish I could radiate to every human soul what I mean by having one's mind, one's soul, live in the open. Words fail to convey what I mean. The sense of largeness, of expansion, of breadth, depth, width, and height are as tangible in soul-results as in those of body. None can live in the open all the time and become sordid money-grubbers. If they are to become rich they do it in a large, expansive, virile way that commands respect. It is only the shut-in man that can add to his millions by cheese-paring methods, by grinding the face of the poor, by counting up cents and nickels and dimes wrung from the labor of the children of the poor.

Read these lines from a wonderful poem of the out-of-doors by Edwin Markham, and see how much you can make it mean to yourself:

> I ride on the mountain tops, I ride;
> I have found my life and am satisfied.

> I ride on the hills, I forgive, I forget
>   Life's hoard of regret—
>   All the terror and pain
>   Of the chafing chain.
>
>   Grind on, O cities, grind;
>   I leave you a blur behind.
> I am lifted elate—the skies expand;
> Here the world's heaped gold is a pile of sand.
> Let them weary and work in their narrow walls;
> I ride with the voices of waterfalls!

>   I swing on as one in a dream—I swing
>   Down the airy hollows, I shout, I sing!
>   The world is gone like an empty word!
>   My body's a bough in the wind, my heart a bird!

Never in a thousand years can one get such pure, sweet, pulsing, living and stay-long-with-you delights as these, in a city. Granted there are pleasures in the ballroom, and they are doubtless great, but can they begin to compare with the delights of out-of-doors? Languor next day, ennui, jealousies, heart-burnings, gossiping, cruel slandering, ruination of health, too often come with these city pleasures. Then, too, the ballroom in its desirable form is only for the rich, while the poor may enjoy everything good of the great out-of-doors. The city has its theaters, operas, concerts, lectures, and the like, but they are generally at night, compelling people to be out when they should be in bed, turning day into night, and reversing the natural order of things. And the artificial is never equal to the real, the unnatural to the natural.

Then, too, the out-of-doors is such a teacher; and not a teacher of the arid, formal, dry, embalmed knowledge, but the real living facts. As Robert Louis, the well-beloved, says:

> There is certainly some chill and arid knowledge to be found upon the summits of formal and laborious science, but it is all round about you, and for the trouble of looking, that you will acquire the warm and palpitating facts of life.

Book knowledge can never equal living knowledge. He whose mind is stored with what he has read too often only thinks he knows, while the one whose facts are gained at first hand from the real objects themselves knows that he knows. A man in a factory as a rule, in these days of specialization, is only a cog in a wheel, a part of a great machine. Be he a woodworker, he does not make any complete piece of furniture. He saws on one part; another on another; a third on still another; a fourth, who knows nothing of shaping the parts, assembles the whole, and a fifth puts them together; a sixth sandpapers; a seventh stains or varnishes; and an eighth polishes and finishes. So with watchmaking and everything used by human hands. Nobody, nowadays, has the joy of "doing it all."

But in the country a man plows, harrows, sows the seed and cultivates, and during it all he is in the open, seeing all the wonderful phenomena of Nature pass before him in everchanging panorama each hour. That is, of course, providing he has not been ground down by too many hours of hard physical labor until he has become a mere "brother to the ox," and the stolid and stunned creature so powerfully described by Edwin Markham in his *Man with the Hoe.*

Every man needs something both of the city and the country. Rubbing up against his kind sharpens his wits; often makes him more selfish and indifferent to the rights and needs of others; and again prepares him more thoroughly to enjoy what the country offers. So, city man, with all your senses sharpened by contact with mankind, go out into the country to get your soul enlarged. For Nature is the great soul expander.

Read John Muir's *Mountains of California,* and see how the out-door-life enlarged him, made him bigger, grander, nobler than he could ever have been had he stayed in the narrow confines of a city's walls. In one chapter he tells of his experience in a storm in a Sierra forest. Perched high on the mountains a great storm swept over the range. Most men would have remained indoors, afraid of the fierceness of the wind and the beating of the rain. Not so he! There were experiences to be had out there that could come to him in no other way; so out he went. After scrambling through underbrush, climbing hilly slopes, until his blood was fairly a-tingle in response to the power of the storm, watching the swaying of the trees, hearing the crash, every few moments, of a falling tree, he finally decided to see the whole thing from the top of a tree. So selecting a suitable tree he climbed to its topmost branches, and there, swaying to and fro like "a bobolink on a reed," he watched the wind playing with the gigantic trees and the tiny leaves, and listened to such an æolian concert as few men have ever dreamed of.

John Muir's experiences and development are not peculiar to him. Most men who live the larger out-of-door life, who engage in out-of-door occupations have a largeness and expansion about them that is stimulating and inspiring. Read the life of the fishermen—the Gloucester Folk, and the Folk of all the shores of the sea, who gain their livelihood by battling with storms and circumventing them. What brawny arms and shoulders and backs; what tremendous power; what deep breaths in powerful lungs! See the pilots who come out to meet the transoceanic steamers; what brave, powerful, massive men they are! Ordinary men are dwarfed in their presence—not merely physically, but mentally and spiritually. See the captains of these same great steamers, and all sea-going vessels, and the very sailors; there is a strength of body and a largeness, an openness of disposition, that is good to come in contact with. Who that has climbed the Swiss mountains with an Alpine guide but has felt the strength and power developed by ages of conflict with snowstorms, avalanches, and other great Nature forces. Even the loggers in the forest swing their axes or handle the huge logs with an ease and power that stagger the ordinary city man. Think how the old time stage-drivers used to handle their six- and eight-horse teams with ease and elegance, guiding and directing their movements as gracefully as a *grande dame* promenades in her ballroom. Who has not been thrilled with the doings of the live-saving service, and the lighthouse keepers? What city girl could have dared do as did Grace Darling, the lighthouse keeper's daughter, who insisted upon her father rowing with her to rescue a shipwrecked crew in the face of a howling storm? What delights I myself have enjoyed out on the plains, prairies, and foot-hills, riding with the cowboys. Well do I remember several *rodeos* I united with in Nevada, where we rode madly after the wild cattle and horses, over and through the sagebrush at break-neck speed, now dodging to the right, now to the left, now jumping a piece of brush that could not be dodged. We went up hill like the wind, and then started down hill at equal or greater speed, and once, getting into a grove of trees, I had to learn to bend down flat on the horse's back to avoid being swept off. "Let your horse go where he will. He understands his business, and you don't," were the instructions I had received, and well it was that I was not required to guide my animal. I had enough to do to keep my seat. Talk about rough-riders! I was soon a rough-rider, indeed. And how tired out and weary I was that night, but how I slept! I had been dyspeptic, sleepless, and anæmic. Three weeks of this shook me up so that my liver worked as it had never worked in my history before. I got until I could eat and digest anything, and my sleep was sweet, sound, dreamless, and refreshing. Would that I had had sense enough then and there to resign the pastorate of my church; quit being an indifferent and unhealthy parson; become a cowboy and gain health, vim, vigor, strength, life.

I suppose I had to come to it slowly, but come I did to the most important facts, viz.: that I could never be healthy indoors, and that I must live in the open. And as I got out more my intellect and spirit expanded as my body grew healthier, and I began to learn more from the objects around me than I had from all my schooling, all my books, and all my theological training and study.

Nowadays there is no out-of-door occupation that does not appeal to me; a ditch-digger, a navvy on a railroad, a roustabout on a dock, a deck-hand on a steamer, a brakeman, a road mender, a plowman, a carter, a teamster—even these, the lowliest of the out-of-door callings, show to me men of rugged strength that delight and appeal to me.

How one's very soul thrills in sympathy as he thinks of the marvelous achievements of the great explorers—all of them men of the out-of-doors; Columbus, Magellan, Capt. Cook, Kane, Sir John Franklin, Peary, Sven Hedin, Capt. Burnaby, Burton, Livingstone, Stanley, Major Powell, and a host of others. How the mere thought of them and their lives radiates the very spirit of energy, strength, courage, daring, independence, self-reliance! In their physical or spiritual presence you feel you are in contact with an entirely different set of earth's mortals than ordinary men, for they radiate unconsciously the largeness, the expansiveness, the majesty and strength of the vast out-of-doors.

Rudyard Kipling in his *Captains Courageous* fully explains what I mean about this largeness and nobleness of soul that come from the out-of-door life, in telling of the fishermen of the New England coast. In his vivid English he pictures their daily life, what their work is, how they have to brave the perils of the deep, the dangerous fogs, the uncertain storms, the sudden death that comes when a great vessel looms through the fog and cuts them down. Yet they go ahead as a matter of course. Their life enlarges their faith and trust; either it is that or they become used to looking in the face of danger and death and then calmly continue in their work. No man does this without deepening and broadening his life.

When it comes to gardeners I fairly envy them. Think of the wondrous life that is theirs. To learn and know the life-habits of plants and flowers, and to see them growing from tiny seeds, or slips, or cuttings into all their rich and perfect beauty. I never knew a despondent gardener. His profession forbids it; his experience rebukes it. So of late years, in my crude way, I have been trying to become a gardener, when I am at home and have time.

What an unspeakable joy there is in all this work. How it occupies one's brain and body, and drives away all despondency, care, blue-devils, and worry. Out in the garden I am a king, a proud monarch, robed in blue flannel shirt and overalls, my scepter a spade, and my right to rule demonstrable by my strong muscles, steady nerves, strong lungs, healthy skin, and clear eyes. Who would not reign in such a realm?

More than all else I feel when living this life that I am lifted above all the petty meannesses of men and women. I am dealing with creative forces—things direct from the hands of God—sunshine, air, water, soil, growth, development, life. And how such feelings expand the soul!

Then I begin to think of the wonderful work in flowers, fruits, and plants performed by Hugo de Vries and our own Luther Burbank, and as I recall their achievements I feel the opening up of a new realm before me. Never can I forget the joy of a couple of days with Burbank at his home at Santa Rosa, and his "proving grounds," at Sebastopol. I there saw his winter rhubarb, and as we walked along we came to his cactus patch. The first section was of the rude, prickly leaves I was so familiar with on the desert; the next section less prickly and so on, until at last, with a frolic, Mr. Burbank "dived" into the cactus, rubbed his face and ears against the great leaves and demonstrated them free from every vestige of a thorn.

Then we saw flowers that he had completely changed, in size, color, form, and odor, and when you ask how it was all done he declares that any man or woman with the necessary patience and skill (and skill comes with patience) can produce results as apparently marvelous as his own. For the marvel is apparent and not real; it is nothing but the understanding and application of natural laws; laws that Darwin and others have well understood and enunciated.

At Sebastopol I had the joy of seeing him work in the selection of plum trees. Row after row of young bearing plum trees stood before us. With two men following him, one with black strings, and the other with white, he began. Picking a plum from the first tree, he bit into it. I did likewise. To me it seemed a good plum. He rapidly commented upon: 1, its appearance, shape, etc.; 2, color; 3, firmness of texture; 4, flavor; 5, sweetness. Then he did the same with the tree: its extent of foliage, shapeliness, etc. All these things had to be considered. The first few trees he took very slowly and deliberately in order that I might clearly comprehend what he was after. Then, almost as quickly as his eye fell upon a tree, he had put his teeth into the fruit, his trained intellect had decided whether the tree was worth keeping or killing, and as he said "keep" or "kill," the attendants tied on the corresponding white or black strings. To produce the plum he wanted he assured me he has destroyed over a million trees.

His apple trees are perfect marvels. Some of them bear upwards of two hundred different kinds of apples, and he says it is comparatively easy to produce an apple of any color, texture, size, flavor, and sweetness desired.

Think what Nature has taught to such a man. He is not what you would call a supereducated man in books; but he has read Nature as few men in the history of the world have done, and she has revealed many of her most intimate secrets to him. And as you talk with him you find in this quiet, unassuming, sweet-spirited, gentle-hearted man a breadth, a largeness, a sweep of soul that are rare.

And Nature gives this same largeness to a woman as well as a man. Women who get into the bigness of the out-of-doors get away from feminine pettinesses just as surely as men do from their narrownesses and prejudices. I have two women friends in California (or had, until one passed on), both of them expert and scientific florists. One lived at San Buena Ventura, and the other at San Diego. The names of Mrs. Theodosia Shepard and Miss Kate Sessions are known throughout the world. Both women determined to devote their lives to a scientific study, *out in the garden*, of plant life, and each has therefore done things, achieved results that have made her world-famed. How much better this, than to live the narrow, contracted life of most women.

Another woman friend, Mrs. Sarah Plummer Lemmon, wife of the well-known botanist, and herself a botanist known to the whole scientific world, for years accompanied her husband in his expeditions throughout the wildest parts of Arizona, New Mexico, California, and Mexico. I doubt whether there is a person living who has so real and intimate a knowledge of all this country as has this brave and intrepid woman, who, when Apaches were on the warpath, calmly and steadfastly sustained her husband in his scientific work. In storms and perils, in danger from wild animals and wilder men, away from all luxuries and comforts and often deprived of what most people call necessities, this woman communed with Nature and has thereby grown into a large, commanding, powerful, all-embracing soul, as much above the average woman in intellect as an athlete is above a baby.

I am no technical botanist, yet I have had pleasure untold when wandering in canyon, mountain, plain, forest, seaside, and desert in seeking to learn all I could of the flora of the region. When botanists said that the *cereus giganteus*—the giant suahuaro—was not to be found in California and I knew I had seen it growing on the California side of the Colorado River, there was great pleasure in photographing the few specimens I knew in this habitat and then in hunting for more. How well I remember one day climbing up hill and down, over rocky ridges and dangerous trails and places where there were no trails at all, every now and again seeing fresh specimens, *in California*, of this cactus "that did not grow in California." And when, at last, I stood on a ridge, looking down into a secluded canyon, where there were a dozen or more (which I photographed), I felt as if, humbly though it was, I were being used as an instrument for increasing the botanical knowledge of the world.

CHAPTER XII

RADIANCIES OF JOY, INSPIRATION, AND SERENITY

I want to radiate the healthfulness of joy. Joy is the sunshine of the soul. Let it shine. If there is so much of it that it fills the soul, it makes of it a luminous body that must radiate light and warmth and health to others. The joyous man is the healthy man, and he that has health should joy to give it to others, whenever and wherever he can. My friend, Marshall P. Wilder, was a radiating center of joy as well as fun. He was funny, but he was more —he was joyous. There was no enmity, no malice, no unkindness, no cruelty in his fun; it was all healthful, kind, sane, and joyous.

A little girl once said of a certain man: "I like that man because he always *shines* at me." Don't you want to shine and make glad the innocent heart of a child, the striving heart of the young, the sorrowful and vexed heart of the middle-aged, and the weary heart of the old? Well did Robert Louis Stevenson say:

> A happy man or woman is a better thing to find than a five-pound note. He or she is a radiating focus of good will; and their entrance into a room is as though another candle had been lighted.
>
> There is no duty we so much underrate as the duty of being happy. By being happy, we sow anonymous benefits upon the world, which remain unknown even to ourselves, or when they are disclosed, surprise nobody so much as the benefactor.

Make the most of your happiness, and the least of your sorrows. Use the telescope at the enlarging end for the former and at the reducing end for the latter, until you have learned what most of us have to *learn*—how foolish and wrong it is to make our joys mere *incidents* while we make our sorrows *events*.

I want to radiate a joy in the little things of to-day. Most people live in anticipation. The things of to-day are not enough. It is, "Oh, tomorrow—

next week—next year—will surely bring me my heart's desire!" Let us learn that *to-day* is the fulfillment of the heart's desire. Take to-day *all* it brings, and it will make *to-day* so full that you will have no care for the joys of anticipation. Live *now,* so intensely, so fully, that life *to-day* will be compelled to deliver up all its treasures *to-day*. Hence every day becomes a perfect joy.

I want to radiate *inspiration.* I do not believe the idea that the saints of old who wrote "the Bible," are the only examples of inspiration. God inspires every good man and good woman, and all good in all people comes from Him, for He is the original source.

A self-centered life is a selfish life; a life that gives of itself freely and fully to all with whom it comes in contact is a life of inspiration—it is a radiating center of inspiration. It inspires to courage, to higher endeavor, to larger achievement. I need all this for myself, but I also long and desire to inspire it in others. Many a life seems to have inspiration for the carrying out of its own dreams, ambitions, desires, but none to give away. Yet the lives we touch may need just the impetus, the propelling force—light or vigorous—that we can give to enable the fulfillment in them of half dormant ambitions for good, the attainment of noble endeavor.

What would become of the chick in the egg if the mother hen did not brood over it? She forgets her own desires to move about in the stronger desire to bring into active being the hidden lives within the eggs. Let us "brood" over the souls of men and women, young men and maidens, boys and girls, and quicken to life the dormant powers of the weak, the tender. Aspirations may have begun in them that can only be quickened by warmth and love from outside. Oh, for wisdom, as well as love, to "brood" aright.

This implies a reaching out to others. It means an ability to feel even the hidden or only half-felt thoughts of others, and love and sympathy alone are delicate enough instruments to thus feel. The seismograph, that registers the oscillations of the earth's crust, is one of the most delicate of man-made instruments, yet the human heart that would respond unerringly to every beginning of aspiration and longing for good in every other human soul must be ten thousand times more sensitive than the seismograph. Such a sensitive instrument let each seek to become. We should hear the faintest beat of the human hearts near us and try to inspire those faint beats until they are strong, regular, powerful, certain.

Lives often possess, unknown to themselves, the germ cells of great powers and lofty ambitions that will never be developed unless some outside influence impregnates and vivifies them into existence. With thousands of people the seeds of good in their souls need to be quickened from the outside, and the help, the food, the desire to feed, must also be given from the outside, until they are born and nurtured into active, self-reliant existence. To be this outside quickening power is to be a radiant source of inspiration.

In this connection I have found that every life that is growing, expanding, enlarging, is a stimulation to every other life to grow, expand, enlarge. I seek, therefore, to radiate growth by my own growth. By *being* something, *doing* something, I want to help others *be* and *do*. Growth is the most natural thing in the world, but unfortunately, men and women are far from being natural. How then can I best radiate the inspiration for growth in them? By being natural myself—throwing off the artificialities, the restricting and restraining bands that prevent the best of myself from coming forth—by being real. This demands that I think for myself, that I decide for myself, that I act for myself. Once get into this habit and growth is certain and sure. The storms may beat upon such a life but, like the sturdy oak, it is thrusting its roots deeper into the soil in every direction—it is living for itself—and storms and tempests only make it the more sturdy and strong. This, in its turn, quickens other lives to growth, to self-thought, self-decision, self-action. Too long the leaders have tried to lull the power of thought in the masses. The church has said: "We will think for you on matters of religion. Accept what we teach or your immortal souls will be imperiled." The bar and bench have said: "In matters of law we will decide what you must think and do. If you differ from us your acts will be illegal." The colleges of physicians and surgeons have said: "We will think for you in matters of health. If you differ from us your bodies will become diseased and die." The schools and universities have said about everything: "Think as we teach you, for we have all knowledge and wisdom, and knowledge will die with us," and the result is that to find a being who *dares* to think and decide and act upon his own thoughts is as rare almost as to find a dodo. Thought is for you; growth is for you as well as for all the universe of

God. Teach yourself to think for yourself as naturally and unconsciously as you breathe for yourself. Once and forever rise up in your manhood, or your womanhood, and say: "Henceforth I will think, and decide, and act for myself without reference to what other people think or say or do." And then you will begin to grow as you never grew before.

Doubtless at first you will grow "scraggly," and somewhat wild. But time and experience will prune you. Better do that than never grow at all. It is perfectly true that the way to learn to grow is by growing. We learn to do by doing. Do not be afraid to reach out for growth because you don't know how. If you reach out, and grow, you will soon learn the best way how.

There is another view-point to this question of growth. We have within ourselves the power to quicken or retard our own growth. Too many of us are lazy, physically, mentally, spiritually—yes, and cowardly. We don't want the trouble of thinking for ourselves. It requires energy and courage. It is so much easier for some of us to accept, to drift, to cast off all responsibility. But growth cannot so come. We must row against the tide to develop our muscles. If we accept what others say and do let it be because our best judgment, after due consideration and personal thought, has decided that it is the wisest and best thing for us to do.

Then, too, many of us do not grow because we are content with what we have. The hindrance to life of smug and ignorant contentment, the dwarfing power of self-complacent assurance, who can tell? This must be shaken out of every mortal before he can grow, and this spirit is by no means found in the ignorant and uneducated alone. Boston and New York, Chicago and Minneapolis, are as full of it as Podunk and Milpitas, Four Corners and Snigginsville. Indeed I do not know but that there is more of it per capita in the great centers than in the country villages. And how it retards growth. The complacent, correctly worded and phrased Bostonian, the haughty and self-assertive, successful New Yorker, is each assured that he has all there is of good to have, and that no good thing can come out of any other place than his. Yet God made other places and speaks to other people, and all should be humble and learn, reverent and grow.

Some do not grow because, having something, they are either too indifferent, too lazy, too cowardly, or too fearful to make extra exertion, to reach out after, to strive for more than they already have. The man who hid his talent in a napkin is a type of this class. Let us arouse from our indifference, our cowardice, our fearfulness, and seek to become something larger, better, more useful than hitherto we have been. To such there is no growing old. Gray hairs may come, wrinkles may seam the face, yet the heart is ever nourished from the fountain of perpetual youth. The life is ever fresh and full of exuberance, and therefore is a radiating center of youth and energy.

The older one becomes in years, the greater should become the growth of the mind and the soul.

> Grow old along with me,
> The best is yet to be;

said Rabbi Ben Ezra, and he spoke the truth. What radiating centers of spiritual growth in others are old men and old women, who have learned the simple secret of constant growth in themselves, which is the secret of perpetual youth.

Growth means fruitage, growth brings flowers. The fruit and flowers of life that nourish, refresh, and delight others come only to those who grow. Roses always come on the new growth; fruit buds best on the new branches; the best grapes are always on the new stems. And the older the bush, the tree, the vine, the more beautiful, the more rare, the more delicate the fruit and flowers.

The life that is growing is constantly searching for nourishment. The leaves of the tree absorb from the sun and the atmosphere, the roots from the soil. If the sun does not shine directly upon the leaf it reaches out, turns around, struggles until it puts itself in proper relation to receive all that the sun has to give. If the root cannot reach the nutriment, the moisture, it stretches and grows up, down, around, over, under, *through* obstacles until it gains that which it needs for life and growth.

Human lives are like trees. They must turn leaves to the sun, send out rootlets and tendrils in every direction, for moisture and nourishment, searching until they find, and demanding until they get all they desire. And the glory of this searching and demanding by the human soul is that there is a whole infinity of space and power, living, palpitant, energized for it to search in. If it search it cannot search in vain. If it demand it must receive, and receive abundantly.

Above *all* things, and in all things, at all times and under all circumstances I would radiate a calm serenity. There is a rich fullness to me that is wonderfully significant in that first line of John Burroughs' *Waiting*. Look at it and let it sink in:

Serene, I fold my hands and wait.

Few are serene, fewer still can wait. We are all in a hurry, we are all impatient, we are easily ruffled. How rare the man or woman of self-poise —the being who has full command of his soul, mind, and body. Anger, jealousy, misunderstanding, backbiting, lying, slander, hate, praise, blame— all alike have no effect in disturbing the beautiful calmness of the serene of soul, who are affable alike to friend and foe, helpful alike to each, sympathetic alike to each. There is no haughtiness in serenity, as some suppose, though there is much pride. Yet it is not the pride of conceit, the pride of power, of possession, of superiority, but the wholesome, joyous, happy sense of a full-flowing life, every good channel of which is healthily full—healthily flowing to healthy ends. *That*, to me, is serenity. The self-consciousness that "all things are working together for good," and working to the full. There is no walking delegate to dictate the length of the hours such a life shall work, or live. It lives for the very joy of mere living, and living means working, giving, doing for others, more than for self.

I can see, dream of, long for, anticipate the possession of, some such serenity, and my ideal of what it is and my reaching after it is what I would radiate, though as yet I am but as one who seeks after rather than as one who has already attained.

Personally I am naturally the very opposite of serene. Physically I used to be easily disturbed. A whisper in an audience of two thousand people would distress me greatly, and render me intensely nervous. I have many a time "called people down," in my own audiences and by sheer force of will compelled silence, and when at concerts, have asked people (not always either gently or kindly) to cease their rude whisperings, yet, at the same time, I never once lost my calmness, the possession of myself, without intense annoyance. I longed to be able to suppress the whispers without a ripple in my own mind or soul, by the sheer force of right, kindliness, courtesy, serenity. The more I possess serenity the more I shall radiate it. It is a priceless boon, to be desired more than great wealth, and, when possessed, to be prized and treasured more than all the jewels of the world.

CHAPTER XIII

RADIANCIES OF THE WILL

There are three things I wish to radiate as to my own will. We speak of men being self-willed, strong-willed, weak-willed, and the like, but at the outset I wish to radiate my desire to be "Divine-willed." By this I mean I wish to recognize the world-wide—nay, the universe-wide—difference between the great, all-powerful, all-wise, all-beneficent, all-harmonious *will* of the Great Creator, and the oftentimes foolish, weak, wavering, irresponsible, ignorant, mistaken will of the human being. Every real man and woman wishes his, her, life to be a useful life, a life that accomplishes something, and that something must be "worth while." It is essential, however, if one would accomplish this that he start right. Now, here is the crucial question—How can you know that you are right? The answer to this question is what I would put into every young man's and young woman's heart—into every boy's and girl's heart—so that, at the start, he, she, may be sure a right start is being made. *The only sure way is to drop your own will and become "Divine-willed."* This by no means signifies that you become a nobody, a cipher, an insignificant ant in the world. It is just the reverse. It is allying yourself with the right, the only right, the perfect right, the unchangeable right. Suppose the case that a man starts out in life with the determination to be self-willed about the multiplication table. He insists upon his freedom, his individuality, his self-will, and refuses to be tied to any table made by any one else, be that one God, angel, or man. Who cannot see that such a man is a fool? It is impossible to reject, to "buck against" the multiplication table. Every man, sooner or later, has to swallow it, accept it wholly, completely, unreservedly, live by it, swear by it, die by it, and more than that he has to do it gladly, willingly, or it can never be a real part of himself. If he is all the time protesting against it, and declaring that it ought to be changed or abolished, or not quite so dogmatic in its assertions, he will all the time be worried, distressed, irritated, because it pays no attention to his wishes. Two times two make four, no matter who kicks, or is irritated, or wishes it to be changed, and so with every other statement of the whole table.

What I am getting at is this, that, though we may not always see it at first, or even at second or third sight, the moral world is governed by a multiplication table as sure and certain, as unchangeable and fixed as is the mathematical world. And it is the acceptance of the moral multiplication table that I call being "Divine-Willed." A man may live for years swindling his neighbors and giving them fourteen ounces for a pound, and think he has fooled the multiplication table as easily as he has fooled his customers, but the rate never changed; it was sixteen ounces all the time. A man may fool his neighbors and himself in regard to the *moral* multiplication table, but sooner or later, here or hereafter, in this incarnation or some other, he will have to learn to accept, love, and live by it in every act, thought, and word. It cannot be any other—there is no other door—this is the only salvation. *This* is accepting Christ—the Truth, the Way, the Life, living the Life He lived, filled with the Divine-Will, the Divine Spirit, that filled him. Whether you are a gambler, a sport, a liar, a cheat, a Sunday-school superintendent, a fool, a drunkard, a senator, a professor of religion, an agnostic, a wise man or a mere child in knowledge, you can never enter the Kingdom of Joy, Peace, Blessedness, that we call Heaven, unless you conform to the Divine Moral Multiplication Table. This is what I am endeavoring to radiate—that I am trying to set aside my imperfect human will, which sometimes kicks against the unchangeable and immovable, and accept the perfect, complete, and unchangeable.

But you ask: How am I to know this moral multiplication table? Easy enough. Don't try to take it all in at once. Begin at the beginning. Learn the "twos" first. Twice one are two, twice two are four, twice three are six, and so on. Start on the Ten Commandments. Master and *live* them. Then absorb the Golden Rule. Then try the Sermon on the Mount.

There's enough to keep you busy for a few days, anyhow. But I suppose some of you will say you can't do it. Nonsense! You've got to do it, and you won't *really* live until you do. You can't dodge the multiplication table; nor can you dodge these. There is no escape. Divinity never made any man or any woman who could get away from them. Creeds, church dogmas, men's ideas about religion or what they call religion may be true, or may not be true, but the fundamental principles of the life of the Spirit always have existed, always will exist, and every man, sooner or later, must come into perfect harmony with them. This is what I want to radiate—my desire that I should become Divine-willed and that every one else should be the same—quick, soon, now.

Then, having *started* right, one may have more confidence and assurance in taking the next step, which is the second thing connected with the will that I would radiate, viz.: I will to be good for something. What is the purpose, the object of life? What are we here for? To eat and drink, sleep and satisfy our appetites and then die like other mere animals who do the same thing? I don't believe it. I never did. As Browning puts it, a spark has disturbed my clod, and now I am discontented to remain a clod—a mere brute beast, living, as does the hog, merely for the satisfaction of my physical senses. I feel higher, nobler, worthier aspirations within me. John Muir, the great California Nature-lover, scientist, and poet, wrote when he was twenty-seven years old a letter in which he said:

> A lifetime is so little a time that we die ere we get ready to live. I would like to go to college, but then I have to say to myself "you will die ere you can do anything else." I should like to invent useful machinery, but it comes "you do not wish to spend your lifetime among machines and you will die ere you can do anything else." I should like to study medicine that I might do my part in lessening human misery, but again it comes "you will die ere you are ready, or able to do so." How intensely I desire to be a Humboldt, but again the chilling answer is reiterated. But could we live a million years then how delightful to spend in perfect contentment so many thousand years in quiet study in college, so many amid the grateful din of machines, so many among human pain, so many thousands in the sweet study of Nature among the dingles and dells of Scotland, and all the other less important parts of our world.

Here were four noble and beautiful aspirations. 1. To go to college and learn more. 2. To invent useful machinery. 3. To study medicine that he might lessen human misery. 4. To be a Humboldt and explore the world for the enlightenment of mankind.

What do *you* want to be?

To go to college to have a good time (!)—save the mark—as some students do? I was once riding on a railway train going to Boston, and at New Haven twenty-seven young students got on board and every one drunk. Do you think Muir had anything of that kind in mind when he said he wanted to go to college? At one of the great universities of the West I was present when the students made a great uproar because the faculty had prohibited beer-wagons from coming upon the campus to deliver their wares at the "frat" houses. I have seen university "men" celebrating some baseball or other victory when the celebration has taken the form of a drunken and sensual orgy. Can you imagine a man like Muir ever having wanted to engage in such a disgraceful and degrading scene?

Muir started out right. He began by seeking to be "Divine-willed," and then by willing to be "good for something."

A friend of mine, who radiates love and helpfulness to every human being no matter how low and degraded, once helped a poor, ugly, besotted son of the gutter, who had sunk about as low as he possibly could sink. One day as he sat on his piazza enjoying the beautiful calm of a glorious spring afternoon he saw his protégé approaching. Giving him a glad welcome the two were soon in conversation and the gutter-waif finally expressed his thanks for the help and encouragement he had received, and, as is natural with every really awakened soul, wanted to *do something* in return for what he felt my friend had done for him. In vain the helper of men protested there was nothing he wished to have done, but the one who had been helped kept on insisting that he must do something. He said, "I not only want to be good, but I want to be *good for something*. Now, what can I do?"

"Well," at last said my friend, "since you must do something, go out and find somebody worse off, lower down, more needy than you were when you first came to me, and help him."

As he went away my friend settled down to an afternoon's study and enjoyment of his books, and of Nature, but within an hour his protégé returned wearing a smile that reached almost from ear to ear. As he entered the gate he called out: "I've got him! I've got him!"

"Got who?"

"Why, the man you sent me for!"

"What man?"

"The man you told me to go and find and help. I've found him, and I thought I couldn't help him better than by bringing him to you."

"Where is he?"

"He's waiting out here by the barn, for I couldn't persuade him to come up until I had first seen and told you."

"Bring him along!"

As the two derelicts returned, the one towing the other up the walk, my friend said the sight of the second vagabond and outcast was almost too much for him. He was not only ragged and filthy, but thin to emaciation, with that horrible look of long continued debauching degradation. The principal feature about him was his nose—the large, red, pimply nose of the habitual drunkard. Almost instinctively the *lower* human in my friend asserted itself. It rebelled against having anything to do with so vile-looking and disgusting a wretch. "What's the use?" he exclaimed, almost aloud.

Then, suddenly, these thoughts came: "Inasmuch as ye did it unto the least of these my brethren ye did it unto me." "This man is as much a child of God as I am. The *real* man in him is as Godlike as I. He is my brother. We are both sons of God." "And," said he, "I instantly arose and went to meet him, with outstretched hand of cordial welcome."

To shorten the story I can only relate how, after he had had a hearty meal and a long conversation, the outcast finally poured out his soul to the man who had met him as a brother.

"I was not always what you now see me. I was in a good position, honored, respected. Had a beautiful family, a good home, was the superintendent of a Sunday School, the leader of a church choir, and happy in my home, my church, my friends. But I was tempted and fell. I ran away from home and all my responsibilities, and went on falling lower and lower, until this very morning I vowed that the next fall would be into the river or a suicide's grave. But God must have meant me for something or He would not have taken the trouble to get me here this morning. I'm going to try to rise."

With cheering words he was heartily and sincerely encouraged, with neither rebukes nor cant. As he rose to go, he said, "What can I do for you to show my gratitude for what you have done for me?" and he would not take "No" for an answer. He was finally told he might mow the lawn if he chose, and in telling the story, my friend said, with tears in his eyes: "He was so sincere that he went over it four times. He really seemed to have shaved, instead of mowed it." He was then allowed to take a bath, and my friend fitted him out as well as he could with an old suit of clothing. In the meantime a couple of hundred friends who had been invited for an evening open-air social chat and singing began to arrive. The organ was brought out from the parlor, one of the number began to play, and then my friend called for a volunteer choir to come and surround the organ to lead the singing. To his great surprise the bathed and reclothed outcast gently sidled up with the rest. Some of the elegantly dressed ladies looked upon him with suspicion and some fear, which, however, dropped away in great measure, as he began to sing. For, strange to say, though he afterwards declared he had not sung a note for several years, the assertion of the purpose to live a new and clean life, seemed not only to bring back the desire to sing, but actually gave him back his voice. His rich clear tenor soared sweetly and without effort over the voices of the others and then blended perfectly with them in glorious harmony.

A week later, when the friends came, he was there again, and the short seven days of new resolve and high endeavor had so changed him in appearance that no one knew him again. A job had been found for him, and this was done in a remarkable way. Without seeing him, a gentleman, filled with the helpful spirit, and desirous of being good "for something," at my friend's request interested himself in finding him occupation. His capacity was so quickly proven that he was put into a responsible position where a two-thousand-dollar bond was required, which he supplied. He worked so thoroughly and efficiently that he was soon promoted, and ere many months had gone by his family, so long separated from him, was with him in happiness and content. Before a year of service he gained the special reward of $1,000 given each year by the firm that employed him for the highest general efficiency shown in any department, and is to-day honored, respected, back again in the high estate from which he had fallen, but a far wiser, nobler, and better man.

Through tribulation and sorrow, pain and woe, wretchedness and despair, sin and its consequences he had learned the lesson, that you cannot shirk the moral multiplication table—that there is no short cut to goodness, except to accept at once, instead of later, the will of the Divine.

Go back for a few moments to the first outcast, who brought this second one to my friend. Had he gone away with the thought that now he must make some money, he must take care of himself *first*, the second man might have filled a suicide's grave. He started out right—to be Divine-willed—to be unselfish, to be helpful to the rest of the world, and those worse off than himself. Muir didn't want to study medicine to become a great physician for the purpose of making money, but to relieve the pain of unfortunate sufferers. He willed to be good "for something." This is the spirit, the life, I would radiate on every hand, every day. I do not mean that all endeavor for self-improvement, self-culture, self-benefit is undesirable. By no means. But the nearer it approximates to the unselfish ideal, the better it will be. When Walt Whitman was a young man, he was a house-builder. He happened to strike a "building boom," and made money so fast that, said he, "I was in danger of becoming rich." And he decided to go and be an unpaid nurse in the Union Army, rather than spoil himself by becoming rich. To gain riches is good as far as it goes—but it goes a very short way in the road to manhood, character, nobleness of life. So whatever you will to do and be, put a high ideal before you, something immeasurably better than mere money-getting. Make your profession a means of grace, of character-building, of enabling you to benefit and bless the world. Mere financial success can easily be attained, but you will surely not be content with that. Hitch your wagon to a star, and soar upwards. Aim at the high things. Will to do great, noble, beneficent things and that will be willing to be good "for something."

The third thing in connection with the human will that I wish to radiate is what I might term "the insistence of the human will." After I have willed to be "Divine-willed," and to "will to achieve a high and noble purpose," I want to compel my will to keep on willing that which I have already willed. It is comparatively easy to will to do, or be, something, but alas! how far short some of us come from attaining that which we have willed to be. When Jesus sent out His disciples He gave them many warnings, much encouragement, informed them of the difficulties they would encounter, and then incited them to persistence of endeavor by assuring them that "He that endureth to the end shall be saved." It is this thought of "endurance," or "persistence" that I would ever radiate. I have set before me an aim, an object, worthy to be achieved. Though it may be difficult to attain, I will to keep on willing until it is attained.

A short time ago I watched the students at the Physical Culture Training School, in Chicago. It gives me a good illustration of what I would ever radiate.

I saw the leader of one of the classes do a particular act, and then the students, one after another, tried to follow the leader in doing that thing. Some of the men who tried, willed to do it all right, but they did not succeed. Many times a man wills to do a thing when he does not seem competent, but the real man keeps on until he makes himself competent. So with some of these. They went back and tried again—and went back and tried again, and the men who willed and then kept at it until they became competent were the ones that achieved.

One of the great lessons of all life is, not merely to learn to will—that is easy enough—but to insist upon the will keeping at it until we accomplish what we have determined to do. We "will" every day to do things, and yet we do not do them. We say, "I am going to do this; I am going to do that; or the other." We start out in life and we have all kinds of ambitions and aspirations before us, and we say, "This is going to be my achievement; I intend to accomplish this thing." But we get to be twenty-five—thirty years of age, and we have not achieved—that is, the great mass of people have not.

Why?

Because we have not learned this lesson of the Insistence of the Human Will. We have determined to do a thing and then we have not had the power or the courage or the determination or the endurance to keep on willing until the thing desired was achieved.

Let us suppose a case: A man starts in a race; he is on the ground ready to spring forward at the firing of the pistol. The moment the pistol is fired he makes his forward bound and goes ahead as hard as he can. Is a good start all that is needed? I picked up a picture recently of a runner who was coming to the end of his race. His face revealed clearly what a struggle he was having. His mouth was wide open, and he was laboring to the very extremity of his strength and power; he was "enduring to the end." He made a good start, but now at the latter part of the journey the race was more difficult; it was almost dangerous because he was panting so hard he could scarcely get his breath. The whole face, the whole body, seemed in pain and distress; but he was *enduring*; he was going on. It is the man who not only makes the start, but *he who endures* that wins the race.

It is not those who start in with the greatest hope, and faith, and energy, and courage, but "He that shall endure to the *end* shall be saved." It is the enduring to the end. Hence let me urge upon you the speedy learning of this important lesson of life. After you have willed to do a good thing put your purpose before you; keep it clearly, positively in sight all the time; then, every day and every hour, resolve to *do* that which you have *determined* to do; in other words, insist that you do what you have willed to do.

I was once very much interested in watching Bernarr Macfadden, the editor of *Physical Culture* magazine. I was favored with opportunities for coming in close touch with him. The way he insists that his will shall endure; the way he takes himself by the throat, as it were, and insists, is most interesting to me. One day I started out with him for a walk. He was quietly and easily getting himself in training so that he could walk fifty miles and be fresh and vigorous enough at the end of the walk so that he could give a lecture. Certainly it is a delightful and a profitable thing to be able to walk fifty miles without exhausting fatigue. We started out together, but after walking twelve miles I felt weary, and returned. But he went on, and when he returned that night I found he had walked thirty-seven miles. Though he was doing all his regular and arduous work, he was quietly insisting on these long walks, and in a very short time he would accomplish his fifty miles daily with comparative ease. He has mastered the idea—"The Insistence of the Human Will."

Take an inventor. No man ever invents anything unless he insists day after day, in spite of discouragements, in spite of failures, in spite of opposition, sometimes in spite of the stealings of people who would rob him of what he has already accomplished. The man who has the real desire to be an inventor keeps on and on, compelling his will to rewill what he has already willed, and I could fill these pages with the life stories of men who have determined, and of women who have determined, and who have achieved because they have learned this lesson of the insistence of the will.

I once had the pleasure of talking with Thomas A. Edison, in his laboratory, in Orange, N. J. I said, pointing to a mass of interesting looking materials: "What is this, Mr. Edison?" He said, "Oh, I have been working for thirty years on that thing."

"How are you getting along with it?"

He replied, "Well, sometimes I think we are making progress, and then again I think we are not, but the only way we can achieve is by keeping everlastingly at it, and when I can't work, I set my men to work on it, and we are slowly getting results."

And so Mr. Edison every once in awhile astounds the world with some marvelous achievement. People suppose he stumbles on it—that he discovers it in a moment, and perhaps he does, but that moment was made possible by the thousands upon thousands of moments that were as steps he had taken leading up to the place where the vision burst upon him. Do you see the thought? It is the Insistence of the Human Will that compels achievement. It is the man that never lets up that gains the reward.

Fifty years ago a man named Judah set out to survey a railroad across the great Sierra Nevada range of mountains, that vast barrier that seems to separate California from the rest of the world. The people practically said, "You are a fool to think of such a thing," but he calmly replied: "I know I can put a road through; I am going to try it anyhow." So he began to climb those mountain heights. He threaded the passes one by one. He took his men and they worked day after day, week after week, month after month, upon what seemed to be an impossibility.

What was the result? He kept at it until he achieved. He made his plans and made them so well that he ultimately succeeded in convincing the House of Representatives and the United States Senate that such a railroad was possible.

Then four men, Huntington, Crocker, Stanford, and Hopkins, determined to build the road that he had surveyed. Again the pessimists said: "It is impossible; you will never raise the money to build a railroad over the Sierra Nevadas." But the four men worked away, and little by little got the money. As they built they were harassed on every hand. Labor troubles in those days were terrible. The President of the company said, "I don't know what we are going to do." Crocker, the man who had undertaken to see after the actual building of the road, said: "I know what I am going to do; I am going to get help to build that railroad somewhere." And so he sent a man to China to secure a lot of Chinese laborers. These were brought to this country, and the result was that with those Chinamen, in defiance of the President of his company, who had said that Chinamen should not be employed, Crocker built the railroad. And now you can cross the Sierra Nevada range without a thought of care because of the dominant, insistent will of that man and his associates.

The fact of the matter is, if you are going to achieve anything in life you will have to be "drivers"—you will have to keep at it until you succeed. You will have to be a slave driver, and you yourself will be the slave, willingly, gladly, joyously, of your own purpose. Do you want to be a slave to your own purpose? Do you want to *do* the things that you have willed to do? Some of us get the idea that bondage—to be bound to anything—is always an unpleasant thing. Not at all! Bind yourself to a high and noble purpose. Make yourself a slave to it in the sense of conscientiously sticking to it. Now drive yourself, and compel yourself to go ahead and do that which you have determined to do.

When I think of the old pioneers who walked and rode across this country to reach California; when I think of the many dangers, difficulties, and hardships that faced those men; when I see that they were living illustrations of this thought I am trying to bring out—I wish I had only time and space to give a definite account, instead of a mere synopsis of the kind of things they had to endure. They were surrounded by hostile Indians; again and again their lives were in jeopardy. Now and then they came to great sloughs and marshes, and their wagons and animals were bogged. They had to find their way across the dangerous quicksands; hard storms came and they had whirlwinds and floods to contend with. Now and again they found themselves in the heart of canyons, where there was no apparent way out; yet they went on, and on, until they either died or reached the land for which they had started!

A party of eighty set out to cross the great Sierra Nevada range, and the difficulties they encountered can best be imagined when I tell you that forty of them died on the way. The difficulties that beset the forty that were left made it all but impossible for them to get out. One of them told me about the terrible hardships they suffered. She said, "I remember, distinctly, when the time came for us to get away, my dear mother taking up the baby, and leaving me behind with the other baby. She said, 'Now, Virginia, you stay right here!' She then went on with the baby, and, after struggling step by step, in such a way that it would break your heart to think of it, for about twenty paces, she put down the baby and came back for the other baby and myself." And so, step by step, step by step, that woman with her three little children, started on that awful journey of scores of miles through deep snow. Fortunately help came to her assistance and she finally achieved. She reached California, though one would have thought it absolutely impossible. There was the tremendous insistence of the human will.

Let us say "I will!" and then insist upon doing the things we have said we will do.

I remember when I was a boy hearing some one recite something that I thought was very foolish. A little piece of "poetry" it was called. It was as follows:

> Go on, go on, go on, go on, go on, go on!
> Go on, go on, go on, go on, go on, go on!
> Go on, go on, go on!

I have since learned that there is a great deal in that "poem."

CHAPTER XIV

RADIANCIES OF CHEERFULNESS

I want to be cheerful and to radiate cheerfulness at all times, under all circumstances, in all conditions and places. I want to do this because I want to do it. Not because it is my duty, or because I shall make some one else unhappy if I do not, but merely and simply because there is a great joy in the fact of cheerfulness itself.

I have a friend into whose presence I never come without feeling the radiant cheerfulness of his nature. His face lights up with a beautiful smile, his hand is immediately stretched out and my hand grasped with a cordial clasp; kind words come to his lips with a sincerity that one can never question, and in the most unaffected, genuine, and simple manner he radiates the cheerfulness and gladness of his own soul.

Did you never meet with such people who were always bright and sunny, who always gave forth a cheery word, always radiated optimism? Everything they say or do makes you feel with Browning:

    God's in His heaven;
    All's right with the world.

And all this is done without any flattery or conscious effort on their part to make you feel good. Some of the severest rebukes I have ever received were from this man of whom I have spoken, and yet they were given in such a sweet, gentle manner and with such perfect sincerity that not only was there no irritation aroused, but a sense of gratitude implanted that I had such a real, sincere friend.

I do not wonder that men demand cheerfulness in others. It seems somewhat heartless to put up a notice in your office, as I have seen in many offices, "I have troubles enough of my own. Tell yours to the janitor," or as another version has it, "Don't tell your troubles to me, I have enough of my own," yet it speaks of a fact that is all too universal, namely, that each person does have his own large share of burdens which sometimes seem as if they would swamp him.

As Dr. Gulick once wrote:

> There is probably not one person in the world but has tragedy enough and pain enough straight along to warrant—yes, absolutely to warrant—pretty complete discouragement. And I imagine that there is no person who is so perfectly adjusted by nature, so entirely balanced in health, that there are not times when it is necessary to hold himself by deliberate will power— to forget how he has been hurt, to turn aside from some ugly thing in a friend's character, to turn aside from the bad in his own character, for every one of us has that which is bad in his character. Our characters are ugly enough in part so that, if we were to dwell constantly on that part, the prospect would seem pretty disheartening and justifiably so.

All this has to be remembered in our association with men and women. And when we remember, why should we not wish, instead of adding to their burdens, to lighten or help remove them?

That cheerfulness is possible in this world of woe and trial, there can be no question, because every now and again, each of us has met with some person who radiated this quality at all times. And we know that in our own experience, when we have willed to be cheerful and to radiate cheerfulness to others, we have accomplished far more in that line than we otherwise should have done.

Only the other day I picked up a trade journal and in it was a short letter from one business man about another business man who had recently passed away. Let me quote a part of it:

> Away back in the '80's I met him under the following circumstances. I was then in Chicago and although an invalid was well enough to assist my brother a little in his office work.

> One day a stranger came in who received an especially cordial greeting from both my brother and his partner. It proved to be Harry W. Sommers.

He was, for a short time, a daily visitor and when he came in there seemed to come with him a glow of sunshine.

It made the same impression upon me as it does sometimes, after a long period of rain and cloudiness, when the sun, in all its brightness, suddenly bursts forth.

One day he came to bid my brother good-by, and although it is twenty-one years ago, the wave of his hand, the cheery smile and the hearty good-by, as he looked toward me, still linger in my memory.

Many a time since has he come into my mind, although I never saw him afterward, accompanied with the thought that were there more Harry Sommerses in this world, it would be a brighter and far happier place to dwell.

I would far rather leave a legacy like that behind me than to leave an immense fortune over which my heirs would quarrel and go to law and engender ill feelings and then possibly spend in an injurious manner.

It is said of Sister Dora, the noble-hearted woman who gave her life to the iron workers of the "Black Country" in England, that as she went to and fro in the wards of the hospitals, her presence was like a glad burst of sunshine to the poor sick men and women to whom she ministered. Though they were rough, uncouth, even profane and wicked, she never failed in her courtesy and bright cheerfulness, and the result was that patients under her control regained their health far more rapidly than those who were subjected to the depressing influences of moody, cheerless, censorious persons.

The same thing is said of Walt Whitman. When he was in the Government's employ at Washington, with a salary of one hundred and twenty dollars a month, he took forty dollars of this for his own use and spent the other eighty dollars to provide comforts and luxuries for the poor soldier boys in the hospitals. I have heard old soldiers tell of the way they used to feel when he appeared. "It was like the coming of a young Santa Claus." He carried a pack on his back which he would drop by the side of a bed and reaching out his friendly hand, with a radiant smile would say: "Well, how is it with you to-day?" and then, if the soldier were a stranger, he would ask:

"Do you use tobacco?" If the man said, "No," he would reply, "That's good." If on the other hand he said, "Yes," Walt's reply would be the same, and he would dive down into his pack and bring out a little tobacco, which he would give with a few kind and cheery words to the poor bed-ridden soldier. If the invalid didn't use tobacco there was a book, a game, or something else that would bring cheer and forgetfulness. Thus he would pass up and down the wards, radiating brightness and good cheer on every hand. There is no wonder that as he passed outside every eye followed him, every heart felt an instinctive "God bless you," and every voice called out, "Come again, soon."

There surely are enough conditions in Nature to help the soul that wants to be cheerful and radiate cheerfulness. Every morning the sun arises with radiating light, brightness and beauty, illuminating and glorifying even the darkest and dullest of the things of earth. The stars shine nightly in all their sincere and calm beauty, radiating the assurance of Infinite power and perpetual care.

In radiant Nature, the butterfly skims the air in its light and fascinating flight, attracting the eye and charming with its exquisite coloring. The dew of morning, receiving the golden rays of the sun, makes the grass and trees appear as if blossoming in millions of diamonds, each a globe of radiating, scintillating brightness and beauty. The birds sing day and night, rain or shine, in sunshine or storm, radiating their cheerfulness and constant optimism. The trees awaken to the caressing touch of the sun and rustle to and fro, speaking in unmistakable language their joy of mere living, and glistening back and forth their appreciation of the gift of warmth and brightness. The flowers grow as freely in the wilds as in the cultivated gardens of man—blossoming evidences of Nature's power to produce gorgeous and resplendent color, perfection in beauty of form and exquisite deliciousness in odor. Even the snail crawls along expressive of delight in the morning, and the worm comes forth from the clod to express its appreciation.

I have watched the mountains with their snow-crowned, virgin-pure peaks soaring into the blue of the heavens and the massive rocks of the mighty canyons of the West basking restfully in the glorious light of day, and even these majestic rock-giants spoke the unmistakable language of joy, and called upon men to be cheerful.

We find exactly the same spirit and influence, if we will but look for it, in mankind. Too often we see but the sordidness, the greed, the selfishness, the cruelty, the rapacity of men, yet we all know that this is but one side, and it is not the reality, it is only the shadow of the real man, that the *real* man is kind, sympathetic, helpful, generous, true-hearted, and pure. If we fix our eyes upon one tiny spot the size of a dollar that is speckled or black, we can soon shut out all the brightness, beauty, and sweetness outside. I well remember one of the sentimental songs that was current in my boyhood days. It probably had as much of the mock sentiment as any other of these songs, but two lines of the refrain I have never forgotten, and whenever I hear one speaking of the unkindness of humanity, I feel like quoting them:

> But speak not so untruly,
> There are kind hearts everywhere.

In spite of the strenuousness of our modern life, as we look around upon the social settlements, the orphan asylums, and the thousands of men and women who adopt helpless orphans, the prisoners' aid societies, where business men actually make a point of finding their help, where possible, from those who have served a term in prison or the penitentiary, and the thousand and one other institutions which show that the Golden Rule is actively in operation in the hearts of men and women—I say these things make me happy and cheerful, and I feel like singing for joy, that innate beauty is as much in evidence, and more, in the hearts and minds of men as it is in Nature.

So I want cheerfulness to be the constant habit of my mind and soul. I do not wish to be cheerful occasionally or semi-occasionally. I would prefer to be a man of one mood and that mood, with its variations, to be a mood of habitual cheerfulness. I regard a cheerful disposition as one of the most precious possessions. It is like a pair of spectacles that have the power of luminosity within themselves. It sees clearly enough but lightens up the darkest and most dreary spots of earth. Cheerfulness is not only a duty, but a philosophy, a religion, a wisdom. The cheerful man is the perpetually wise optimist. A cheerless or gloomy man is the perpetually unwise pessimist. And years ago I learned to test all philosophies and religions by practical life. No philosophy, no religion was good that could not satisfy every-day life. Optimism never fails at any time, but pessimism is worse than a broken reed to lean upon.

Take the pessimists you know, and I can pretty nearly stake my life upon it you will find nearly all of them dyspeptics, with poor circulation, shivering on a cold morning with their hands in their pockets, complaining that they were not awakened early enough, finding fault because the breakfast was not served just right, railing at the car service, ranting about the rottenness of men in public life. They seem to take a pride in believing, as did Dickens' Mantalini in *Nicholas Nickleby*, that "We are all going to the demnition bow-wows." What a contrast there is between this man and the Cheeryble Brothers of the same book, those great and simple-hearted human reservoirs of cheerfulness and optimism, radiating sweetness, happiness, content, wherever they went, blessing and benefiting every heart willing to accept the sweetness and purity of theirs.

Pessimism is not a working theory of life. It is the substitution of gloomy, deep-blue spectacles for the beautiful luminous ones. As Dr. Gulick says:

> Pessimism is negative, denial, believing that the evil is more than the good, that life is not worth while; it is a dampening down of life. Pessimism tends to its own annihilation, because it takes away life's motives, life's vigor, life's power.

On the other hand, optimism cheers, encourages, brightens, beautifies, glorifies, blesses, helps. And I long ago learned that that man, that woman, who succeeds in helping and benefiting and blessing mankind is essentially an optimist.

The other day I saw the act of an optimist. He and a friend were seated in a street car. It was Saturday night, the car was crowded, and by and by two well-dressed men got in, one of them with an unmistakable look of refinement, the other somewhat coarse looking. Both had evidently been drinking heavily. The more refined and elder of the two could barely stand upright, as the car whirled around the curves. The optimist looked up, saw the state of affairs, and in the sweetest, gentlest manner arose and extended his hand and bade the elderly gentleman take his seat. There was no look of reproach or disgust, and yet I know that he was a rigid abstainer and strong temperance worker and one who hated every form of indulgence in alcoholic liquors. The companion of the man who had taken the seat, began to talk in the ordinary mumbling, rambling, effusive style of the drunkard, and the other without either impatience or any sign of disapproval, quietly entered into the conversation, and I speak only the fact when I state that without any preaching or fault-finding, his few earnest, sincere, optimistic words so won the heart of that large, coarse-looking, drunken man that he seemed absolutely sobered and responded to the higher call of the soul.

This is what optimism and cheerfulness do for mankind, hence I want to radiate it more and more.

Mark Twain was full of this spirit of radiating cheerfulness. In one of his darkest hours in San Francisco, before he had gained name or fame, things had gone wrong and a lady friend passing along a street saw him standing beside a lamp-post with a cigar-box under his arm. "Cigars?" she asked. "Where are you going in such a hurry?" "I'm m-o-o-v-i-n-g," drawled Mark, at the same time displaying the contents of the box which consisted of a pair of socks, a pipe, and two paper collars. Even in his darkest hours he was able to look out upon the bright side, and out from those hours of gloom came some of the brightest pieces of wit and cheerful philosophy to irradiate and bless the entire world.

If I were an employer of labor and could get the right men and women to do the work, I would employ a half dozen for my factory or workshop to teach my employees to be cheerful, to laugh and sing at their work. It would be a good paying investment. I would get a great deal more work out of my employees and of a great deal better quality. A hearty laugh is better than a bottle of medicine; a volume of Mark Twain or Marshall Wilder, better than a library of pessimistic philosophy of high sounding phrases.

Cheerfulness takes the jolts out of the rutty road of life. It is an extra pair of springs to the wagon. It is an automobile shock-absorber. It resists the encroachments of the grouch and bids the blue devils avaunt!

The old-fashioned methods of kings having a clown to keep them and their court laughing during meal time was a profound piece of philosophy and wisdom, for the stomach's sake, if for no other reason. The folly of the clown caused laughter, promoted genial humor which increased the flow of all the digestive juices and thus contributed to good digestion and perfect assimilation. The uncheerful father or mother who sits down to the table like a thundercloud and suppresses the bright, happy exuberance of childhood ought to be taken down to the dentist and pumped full of laughing-gas until he or she would laugh for a week. I would make such people laugh until their sides ached and they had to go to bed to get over it, and every time a frown or gloomy look came over the face I would have somebody lift a warning finger (but also a laughing face) and threaten them with another week's dose of laughing-gas.

"But," says the gloomy one, "life has gone wrong with me. How can I be cheerful when I am out of work and sick and have no friends?" Your case is hard, my friend. I recognize it with sympathy, but let me tell you this, that every grouchy look and word will make it harder for you to get work, and will put friendship further away from you. Even as a business proposition, it does not pay. *Make yourself laugh* and be cheerful, whether you can be or not, for very few men are willing to surround themselves with those who appear to be gloomy, depressed and grouchy. Learn the lesson that it does no good to indulge in self-pity. Whatever the adverse circumstances of life may be, face them like a man.

Years ago I had learned this lesson of refusal to pity myself, and I then wrote:

"I want to radiate a spirit that refuses to pity itself for any of its woes, its afflictions, its misfortunes, its sorrows. There is no weakness so weak as the weakness of self-pity; there is nothing so spiritually debilitating as to brood over one's own sorrows. It is a kind of melancholy selfishness; it neither helps one's self nor others; it is depressing to all concerned. I happened to read to-day in a popular novel a sentence that most truthfully expresses what I believe upon this subject: 'The most absolutely selfish thing in the world is to give way to depression, to think of one's troubles at all, except of how to overcome them. I spend many delightful hours thinking of the pleasant and beautiful things of life. I decline to waste a single second even in considering the ugly ones.'

"It is just as easy to form a habit of dwelling upon the sweet and good and beautiful and happy things of life as upon the bitter and evil and ugly and unhappy things. Brooding enlarges whatever it exercises itself upon, whether it be good or evil, joy or woe. So brood on the good things, cast out the others, and so live that you radiate this joy and determination not to recognize the evil and unpleasant things.

"Self-pity takes the backbone out of one. It robs one of his manhood, his courage, his daring to go on and face all the difficulties before him. It is self-pity that makes the suicide. He looks at his woes, his difficulties, until he cannot bear them, and so goes and takes the big plunge into the dark.

"Brother, sister, quit your self-pitying. There is another side to the darkness. Look up, not down. Remember that, in the words of Robert Browning, 'God's in His heaven, all's right with the world.' So I have long resolved to radiate cheerfulness as much when I am *down*, as when I am *up*—when misfortune glowers upon me, as when fortune smiles. It is so easy to interpret our material good as a proof of God's favor, and our material ill as a sign that He is displeased with us. Those who went to Jesus and asked, when the tower of Siloam fell and killed eighteen: 'Were they not sinners above all others because this thing happened to them?' are not without their myriads of counterparts in the world to-day. When a man strikes a new gusher in an oil region, or a good flow of water in a desert country, or his grainfield gives him seventy bushels to the acre, it is easy enough to believe that Providence is smiling upon him, and, therefore, his faith is strong and unquenchable. I have enough of that kind of faith. I can radiate that without an effort or thought. But I desire above all things to radiate a like sure and definite faith when my neighbor strikes a gusher and I do not; when my *enemy* finds a fine flow of water and *my* crops are being parched—I want as strong a sense of contentment when Fortune *smiles upon the other fellow*, as when it smiles upon me."

This leads to another practical radiance. It is that of absolute certainty that things do not *happen*. There is no such thing as a "happenstance" in the world.

"Nothing happens," is a word often on my inner lips. There is no evil, no wrong, no misfortune to the man who consciously lives with power ever surrounding him. In our short-sightedness, we dream, we think of evil, or ill, or wrong, or misfortune, but if our faith's eyes were always open, we should see nothing but good—and that all circumstances are good in their ultimate results upon us.

Some years ago I met a lady who possessed this spirit of radiant cheerfulness, and yet she was in a sanitarium and had undergone several severe surgical operations.

In conversation with her, I learned that some years before she had found herself afflicted with a tumor in her breast. The surgeon said that nothing but the knife would remove it. This seemed almost like a sentence to death, and my friend and her husband, children, and friends were deeply saddened by the necessity. They all went through a period of deep gloom, of darkness, of despondency. Then there came to her the idea that it was contrary to Nature that she and her loved ones should waste their time, energy, and strength in such repining and sorrow. She remembered the words, "Be careful for nothing, but in everything by prayer and supplication make your requests known unto God," and then there came to her the joy of the promise that followed: "And the peace of God which passeth all understanding shall keep your hearts and minds" in what is sure to be the spirit of peace and love.

So she began to look upon the duty of cheerfulness. She soon saw that it was the only path for her to walk in. The operation was performed. It was serious, and for three years she and her loved ones had to struggle hard to be cheerful and optimistic. But the results more than repaid for the efforts expended, for, when at the end of the three years, the tumor again appeared, even more serious in character, and she had to go to the hospital again, she found that, after the first few dark hours, a great peace stole over her whole being, and as a result of her cheerful radiancy, her husband and children were "adorably cheerful and loving." She has since said:

"I went to the hospital feeling sure that I could find peace in suffering, pleasure in pain, contentment through it all. When I was put upon the operating table this sense of peace and content and lack of fear enabled me to take the anesthetic easily, and after the operation was over, when the pain was terrible, to fight my battle with a happy heart. I faltered a little once or twice when the pain seemed to pile mountains high during the first few days, but when my nurse found that I meant to make the best of everything, she took hold in the right way with a spirit of determination to help me, so it was not long before I really seemed to rise, by means of the very mountains of pain that at first appeared as if they would overwhelm me, to summits of joy, content and satisfaction I could not have known without them.

"As I looked out of the windows, the trees seemed to be putting forth their leaves in richest beauty all *for me*. The birds—the robins and bluebirds—seemed to come and sing *for me*. The air grew daily more balmy and sweet, and as I contemplated these things, I found even the tremendous noises of switching cars and the disagreeable sounds of the engine, combined with the racket of the wagons that came rattling over the cobble-stones, came to be quite bearable. Peace and joy were in my heart. I was content, full, satisfied."

And she certainly looked it. She was a radiating reservoir of these glorious and uplifting qualities. How could she be otherwise? So, with this woman's experience in mind I again urge you to be cheerful. Be happy. Acquire *the habit of the effort*. It soon grows easy. Believe implicitly in the power of Good—and that the apparently bad is contrary to Nature's laws and wishes (being a result of some transgression or ignorance), and that whatever happens is good, for it works out for the best in the end.

And now, to conclude, or as our preacher friends say, "one more word." In my radiancy or cheerfulness, I want to remember to radiate all the time and to all people. It is easy enough to be cheerful in the presence of our superiors and with our companions and equals. But I notice that it is a very different matter with many people to be cheerful with those whom society and the world call their inferiors—the elevator boy, the bell boy, the valet, the chambermaid, the clerk, the stenographer, the laborer, the coachman, in other words, all those whom we call "servants." Many people feel that they are not under any obligation to be cheerful to them, but, oh, what a joy they miss, what a privilege they throw away. Why not especially radiate cheerfulness to the fullest possible extent to those who have less of this world's goods than ourselves? Why not help them bear the burdens of life by your radiant optimism? Let your cheerfulness be real, sincere, honest, manly. Try to concern yourself in their interests and understand somewhat of the battles they have to fight. It does not take up much time or require much effort. It is the *spirit* of the thing that is felt and that counts. So, be cheerful at all times and radiate your cheerfulness to all sorts and conditions of men. Thus you will go through the world leaving a blessed path of sweetness, brightness, and sunshine behind you which will illuminate, cheer, and bless all who walk therein.

CHAPTER XV

RADIANCIES OF MORAL COURAGE

I want to radiate moral courage. Who that has read the life of Emerson cannot appreciate the moral courage that controlled him at all times. He was incapable of cowardice. Timid, sensitive as the most delicate plant, shrinking from notoriety, he yet did and said things that brought down upon him the censure and concentrated fury and hatred of thousands. He, so gentle and kind, spoke words that hit and smashed and crashed through the entrenched ideas of the world like red-hot cannon-balls. Though never a politician, he spoke words on the principles involved in the slavery question that surpassed in fervid eloquence and effective power anything ever said by Wendell Phillips or William Lloyd Garrison. On one occasion he faced a mob of fiery sympathizers with the other side and declared the highest, purest truths of the brotherhood of man, and when remonstrated with for daring such an assemblage he calmly and quietly replied: "Had I been dumb, I would have gone and muttered and made signs."

When men worshiped certain ideas and believed that they were religion, and that it was needful to believe them in order to live aright on earth and win the favor of a heavenly hereafter, Emerson arose and smote them into the dust by the calm, relentless, passionless logic of one who sees and knows—the divinely ordained prophet—and one result of his daring was that he was cast out from his pulpit and from the sweet and hallowed communion he and his grandfathers for eight past generations had enjoyed in the church. What a wrenching of heart strings, what a tearing away of old ties, what an isolation of oneself, what a bringing down of the avalanche of abuse, of slander, of harsh words and unkind deeds! Yet he never hesitated. The oversoul called to the sacrifice, and at the same time pointed to the recompense of the spirit, and he never saw, never knew, never felt the contumely, the scorn, the ostracism, the abuse.

Is it not glorious to live in such a realm of high spiritual courage? To do unconsciously? To *be* unconsciously? Not to have to work your courage up to the daring point; to nerve yourself for the plunge, but to plunge anyhow, trusting, knowing that in doing the highest, the noblest, the best thing conceivable to you, you can never fail? What does starvation of the body mean to the man whose soul is uplifted into the presence of the Most High? Such an one can live for forty days or forty years, if necessary, without more food than would feed a sparrow. What does isolation from his fellows—preachers, doctors, lawyers, every-day men and women—mean to a man who communes daily with angels, archangels, and with God Himself? Does he feel slighted, hurt, neglected? Such a courage as this I myself desire, so that I may live it, radiate it every moment.

It was this courage that made John Brown march on that most quixotic of all marches—with a handful of men to free the slave. It was rebellion, anarchy, unlawful invasion, the breaking of man's law—of course it was. But he saw a higher vision than man's outlook, he felt a higher call than man's demand, and he knew no law of man in the obedience of his soul, body, life, *his all*, to the call of the Spirit. And though a rude Kansas pioneer and farmer, he had the soul-courage to obey. Forward! March! He marched to his death!

Did he? No! He marched to the death of his body, but he began a triumphant march in the heavens forever brilliantly illuminating the minds and souls of men, and lifting them up into a higher state of life, making them less sordid, less afraid of position, life, honor, less easily influenced by the keen censure and scorn of the blind world.

Talk about battlefields and batteries, forts and forlorn hopes and the courages of the Charge of the Light Brigade, or of the Stand of the Old Guards at Waterloo, or of Dewey sailing into Manila Harbor; what were those acts of physical courage compared with the moral heroism that leads a man to dare the stake, the cross, or the tortures of the bigot? Read Mark Twain's *Life of Joan of Arc,* and feel your heart throb to the high-souled, divinely inspired courage of that girl of eighteen; not only physical courage, as when she led, in person, the charges of the French army against the English, who had been victorious in France for almost a hundred years, but when she dared the great ecclesiastical courts that badgered and baited her, as she sat unaided, alone, unbefriended, undefended, unadvised by man, for weeks at a time, when the cowardly hounds were determined to send her to the stake. Where did her heroism and courage come from that she, a mere country peasant child, who had never even ridden a horse, or seen a battlefield, who never had read a book, or knew the first thing of guiding and controlling soldiers, or setting an army in battle array; I say, where did her courage come from, that she could dare to go into the proud presence of nobles and warriors and demand that they give her a guard to take her to the King of France, where she assured him that she would soon drive out the English and have him duly crowned king of his reconquered provinces? Here was the radiant life in actual, potent exercise. She radiated courage and faith, just as the sun radiates heat—in such abundance that men sweated with it, men were fired to the intense heat and fervor of new life and courage with it. So that, from a cowed, disheartened pack of whipped men, who fled from the mere sound of approach of a small body of English soldiers, raw recruits, as well as seasoned veterans, shouted to be led against the foe, and when once in the conflict hammered away regardless of wounds, even of death, until victory was theirs.

Whence came this radiant courage and power? It was simply because she dared to listen to the voices speaking to her soul, and *nothing else counted*. That's the life I want to get hold of. That is the courage and the life I wish to radiate. Afraid of men, of starvation, of opposition, of censure, of hatred, of ostracism? No! Why should we be afraid to lose a few cents, when our hands are filled with diamonds, and rubies, and pearls, and nuggets of gold? Why should we fear men, when we have the courage of our convictions?

Let us look not down, but up, and seek to draw from the heavens above the inspiration, the courage, the bravery, the heroism of the soul.

There has recently passed away in despotic Russia a man whose life for years has radiated moral courage throughout the world. Tolstoi had the courage of his convictions. He felt that social distinctions were wrong. Immediately he did the practical thing—put himself on the plane of every common laboring man by personally becoming a tiller of his own soil. "What a fool!" exclaimed the aristocratic world to which, by birth, he belonged. "Does he think he can change our opinions by that silly act?" they cried. No! He knew it would have little or no effect on them, but he was compelled to clear his own soul. So he braved their laughter and scorn, their contumely and contempt, that the world might know for certain what he really did think and feel.

He came to the conclusion that the Government of Russia, and the conduct of the ministers of the Greek Church—the established church of Russia—were neither in conformity with true religion nor true brotherhood. Though the former was despotic, and the latter as "hide-bound and dogmatic as rigid adherence to dead forms and creeds ever makes men," he fearlessly expressed his inmost convictions against both and called upon them to change, reform, amend their ways and actually become what they professed to be. The state threatened him with Siberian banishment unless he kept silence, but never till death silenced him did he heed the threatening command; the church cast him out, and then he wrote a book, *My Religion*, that gave newer and more exalted conceptions of religion to the world, even though possibly it would be hard to find a single man who accepts everything just as Tolstoi set it forth in that book.

He came to the decision that the fine clothes and luxurious surroundings of the rich and noble were neither Christian nor humane. They caused envy and bitterness in the hearts of those whose lives were one long struggle with poverty. So at once he cast off his gorgeous apparel, denuded his own rooms of all unnecessary and elaborate furnishings, and thus, again and further, placed himself where men could feel the truth and power of his utterances about human brotherhood.

When Russia declared war against Japan, Tolstoi wrote a letter to the Emperor, the state officials, and the Russian people that was a loud trumpet blast heard throughout the world calling upon them in the name of their Creator and down-trodden humanity to stop! and declare peace. Many a man had been sent to Siberia for life—nay, sent to be speedily tortured to death—for far less than this, but this fearless old man let his voice ring out with a power that convinced thousands as never before that war at its best was but a relic of barbarism and a disgrace to every professedly progressive nation.

Oh, for a courage like Tolstoi's—true-hearted, brave, simple-minded, pure, that never failed when called upon. Granted he was "queer," "quixotic," "unbalanced," "impracticable," was not his queerness and impracticability at least on the side of the moral forces of the world? Everybody knew where and how he stood; where his sympathies were; and his life has strengthened the backbone and put new vigor into the weak knees of hundreds of thousands, for moral courage radiates with power that increases according to the square of the distance. It does not grow less; it enlarges; for each man who feels it becomes a new generator and transformer and thus enlarges and increases its radiating power four-, eight-, twelve-fold.

Henry Bergh was another of these heroic moral-courage radiators. His tender heart was cut to the quick day by day by seeing the cruelties perpetrated upon the poor dumb brutes of the city of New York. He determined to do what he could to stop these barbarous practices. He agitated and wrote, spoke and interviewed until he succeeded in getting ordinances and acts passed which gave him power to prevent whatever cruelties he saw. How he was jeered; how he was cursed, when he sought to interfere with a brutal driver who would cruelly whip his horses to compel them to drag loads beyond their strength! The newspapers said he stood in the way of business, and they sarcastically called him "the knight of the doleful countenance," not realizing that it was the cruelties perpetrated by so-called men upon their younger brothers—the dumb animals—that had so frozen the pain and anguish of his heart upon his face. But his heart never failed, his courage never wavered. Threatened, mobbed, his life often in peril, he fearlessly waged constant warfare against cruelty, and to-day the very city that hated and scorned him is building monuments to his honor in every street-watering trough they erect. And his radiant influence has reached every civilized city *in the world,* such is the penetrating radiancy of a loving and true heart.

Before I proceed to a further consideration of this radiancy of a large-hearted, moral heroism, I want to answer the objection raised to what I have already written by a young man to whom I read it. He said: "But I am not an Emerson, or a Wendell Phillips, or a John Brown, or Tolstoi. What chance do I have of exercising moral courage?"

A very pertinent question, and one I am glad to try to answer. I do not believe there was ever a man, a time, or a place which did not, sometime, somehow, call for the exercise of moral heroism. And especially in these days of lax principle, breaking down of old standards, political graft, and worship of material success. What minister is there in no matter what church who is not called upon, now and again, nay, often, to speak fearlessly upon some practical subject upon which people are looking for light? Is he a moral hero who taboos such subjects, who refrains from discussing them in the pulpit because they are not "gospel" subjects? What gospel subject can surpass in interest and in human and divine appeal to the soul of man the "white-slave" question, and a host of other subjects upon which ordinary well-to-do men and women need enlightenment? That minister is endowed with the radiant power of moral courage who, even though he offend some of the smug, comfortably righteous members of his congregation, dares to denounce the church people who rent their houses and lands for immoral purposes, for breweries, for saloons, for any and all things that destroy men's bodies and souls and bring suffering to innocent women and children. Take the child-labor question, especially in the communities where men live who have become rich by using child labor, whether in cotton factories, glass factories, tobacco, or any other factories. Should not such men hear the gospel plainly and without equivocation? Who is to give it? The minister of the Christ who came to seek and save the down-trodden, the injured, the forsaken, the lost. Then all honor to the man who dares to speak out, dares to be true to the inward voice, though he lose caste, position, salary.

The same courage is required of the politician. How often the public clamor for, or against, the very opposite of that which is right. In California a few years ago there was a great fight for the exclusion of the Japanese and Chinese. How about the doctrine of the brotherhood of man? Can we play fast and loose with eternal principles? No! Let the true politician stand by the truth and let the poltroon sacrifice his principles for temporary advancement and gain.

There is not an employee who at some time or another is not called upon to exercise moral courage. Some are asked to do dishonest, mean, disreputable, contemptible things—for their employers. Some have one temptation, some another. Stand firm for the highest truth. Be morally brave and courageous. Dare to refuse. Dare to risk losing your job rather than your character. Dare to be poor rather than mean.

One of the great temptations of men and women to-day is to appear better off than they are. We are all as good as everybody else—so we say—and, therefore, we must dress as well, dine as well, live as well, and show off as much. What is the result in many cases? Financial worry or disaster at best; criminality at worst. For many a man to-day is in the penitentiary because he and his wife did not have the moral courage to dare to live within their income; she did not dare to wear her last-year's hat, or a made-over gown, and he did not dare say No! when she insisted upon having new and expensive things, or would not deny himself when his "set" indulged in an expensive pastime which he could not afford. Oh, the pity of it! Let your courage have a chance to grow. Plant the seeds of moral heroism early, so that when the testing time comes you will find the tree already grown to which you can cling.

Every boy and every girl—no matter how young—has times when temptations come which it requires moral courage to resist. Better teach your boy the duty, pleasure, and benefit of this resistance than have him win every other prize of excellent scholarship. Are you radiating such courage so that your children feel it? That they are influenced by it? Happy you, if you are, for it will return to you in the beauty, strength, nobility, and grandeur of your boy's, your girl's, life in after days to your benediction and joy.

The world is cold for want of moral courage. Turn on the radiator. Call on the great source for a full supply and help make the world warm with the heroism, the bravery, the moral courage it needs.

Possessed in any degree, however small, of this heroism of the soul, I, myself, want to radiate the consciousness that my *natural and proper place is in the forefront of every movement that makes for human progress*. Most men are laggards in human progress. Of comparatively only a few is it said in such things: "He is abreast of his times." Of only the less than few—the solitary, the individual soldiers—is it said: "He is ahead of his times." Here I want to find my place. These are the men and women with whom I would stand. And I would so radiate the spirit of advancement and progress that every awake and alert soul and also every quiescent and sleeping soul will feel and know it when we come in contact.

In November, 1910, there was held in the city of Chicago an anniversary celebration of the life and work of Theodore Parker, a New England Congregational clergyman who lived from 1810 to 1860. When professional philosophers, reformers, and preachers were discussing, in an academic fashion, the question of human freedom, while under our banner of professed "human rights for all," the shackles were on the hands of four millions of slaves, while professional statesmen were temporizing with this iniquitous system and proposing compromises, all of which affected slave owners, and none of them made the slave free, Theodore Parker, in season and out of season at times appropriate and inappropriate, was a flaming firebrand of passionate utterance against the hideous hypocrisy of our national pretense while the rattle of these shackles was in our ears. It was nothing to him that the solid South was against him; it was of no weight to him that many of the "respectable moneyed men" of New England were engaged in the slave trade, and that "practical men of affairs" counseled moderation, toleration, and caution in dealing with so "delicate" a subject. He saw only the horrible facts of human slavery, and that this slavery existed in a land on whose national banner were inscribed the words: "We believe it to be a self-evident truth that *all men* are created free and equal," and the only delicacy he felt was that the national conscience should be aroused to its hypocrisy, self-deceit, inconsistency, and dishonor, and that the slave-holding and slave-trading business should cease in this "land of the free and home of the brave." We, to whom the Emancipation Proclamation has been familiar ever since its promulgation, cannot conceive the terrible stir, the bitter antagonism, the fierce hostility Parker's clear and ringing words caused at the time of their utterance. In vain his fellow-preachers begged him to be more cautious, to adopt a more conciliatory tone. Like Campanello, who took a bell for his crest, and for his motto the words, "I will not keep silent," he quietly but firmly, calmly but resolutely, refused, and rang out all the louder and more insistently his call to the drugged conscience, sleeping honor, and deadened humanities of his fellow citizens. It was he who inspired in Lincoln that memorable phrase made forever world-famed by his glorious Gettysburg speech: "Government of the people, by the people, for the people." Lincoln spoke November 19, 1863. Parker had written in November, 1846, these words:

> Let the world have peace for five hundred years, the aristocracy of blood will have gone, the aristocracy of gold will have come and gone, that of talent will also have come and gone, and the aristocracy of goodness, which is the democracy of man, the government *of* all, *for* all, *by* all, will be the power that is. Democracy is direct self-government over all the people, by all the people, for all the people.

By way of parenthesis, it is interesting here to add that in *The Christian* (a London, England, weekly paper), for September 17, 1910, there was a letter giving an even earlier use of the phrase, as follows:

> SIR: In your report of Principal Carpenter's striking speech at Budapest, you cite his reference to the well-known fact that "It was from Parker that Abraham Lincoln borrowed his famous phrase, 'Government of the people, for the people and by the people.'" But the further fact should be remembered that Parker himself borrowed it—doubtless through his perusal of the current *Monthly Repository*—from Rev. Robert Aspland, our once-famous Hackney minister. It occurs in Mr. Aspland's speech at the great Whig banquet of 1828, which celebrated the repeal of the Test and Corporation Acts, and at which, amongst many distinguished speakers, Mr. Aspland, by common consent, bore away the palm of eloquence.—AN EX-M. P.

These facts in the history of a great phrase I am glad to present, but the most important fact is not the name of the originator, but the names of the men who made the phrase live in the hearts of their fellows as biting, stinging, awakening truths. Parker was one of these. Lloyd Garrison, Wendell Phillips, John G. Whittier, Lowell, John Brown, Lovejoy, Lincoln, were others. And you and I, friendly reader, are to-day basking in the fuller and larger sunlight of freedom let into the house of our common humanity by the fearless, uncompromising, daring courage of these men.

Let us not be laggards in the army of human progress; nor content even to be abreast with the times. Let us be athirst for deeper waters, clearer streams. Let us get nearer the mountain top than either of these two crowds. Let us drink of the fountain spring itself and know nothing else but the fundamental principles of human relationship, and, drinking of them to the full, go forth and radiate them in their original purity, sweetness, and power, diluted only by our imperfect human expression. Let us, in this and all similar matters, make the words of Browning ours, that we may ringingly declare to the world as well as quietly radiate them:

> What had I on Earth to do
> With the slothful, with the mawkish, the unmanly?
> Like the aimless, helpless, hopeless, did I drivel—Being—who?
> One who never turned his back but marched breast forward,
> Never doubted clouds would break,

> Never dreamed, though right were worsted, wrong would triumph,
> Held we fall to rise, are baffled to fight better, sleep to wake.

Let us not merely come in for the rewards of life's conflicts in which the few battle for the rights of the many. Let us be in the forefront of the battle array; even if only as standard-bearers, or buglers, or drummer boys in the forefront of the advance army, and though our hearts are often shaken by human cowardice, let our souls triumph and keep our faces towards the foe, courage at fighting pitch, resolution indomitable, purpose invincible, so that, if fall we must, we shall fall with eyes heavenward, and breast fearlessly exposed to the fire of the enemy.

I know of no conflict now as severe as the fight for the abolition of the slave, yet I am in the fight to help women gain the suffrage, and in the temperance reform. I have been abused by my scientific friends as an anti-vaccinator and anti-vivisectionist; have been threatened with a thrashing several times for interfering with brutal teamsters and others who were cruel to animals and children; have lost caste and position (with a few people) because I would rebuke corporate injustice, greed, and tyranny; I have cast behind me much money because it was offered me in exchange for my independence and freedom. These are small things as compared with the heroic acts of the giants of past days, but they are the deeds my soul has been called to face. And I mention them not in boasting, but as another "declaration of principles," principles I wish to radiate on every hand, under all circumstances, to all people.

For I am anxious and determined that, according to the best of my ability, I will do my share of the work of my time for the benefit of the future. What would we be to-day without the advantages of Magna Charta, of the Bill of Rights, of the Declaration of Independence, of the Emancipation Proclamation? Who won these charters of our liberty? The heroes of the past. Then the questions I constantly ask myself are: "What are you doing to add to these liberties to hand on to future ages? You have received freely; how are you giving? I want to help make the future more glad and blessed, just as my present has been made glad by the actions of the heroes of old. I have been inspired to high resolves, heroic endeavors, blessed ambitions by what they achieved. Am I doing anything to pass on these high inspirations to endeavor and ambition? These men met obloquy, hatred, shame, contumely, contempt, danger, financial loss, physical peril, and in John Brown's, Lovejoy's, and other cases, death, because of their daring advocacy of unpopular movements. Shall I be any the less a man than they? Shall I have received so much, and then be craven and pass on so little?"

I believe that each generation must pay interest *in kind* on all their heritage of the past, or they mark the period of a nation's decline. Unless we are better, nobler, truer, more advanced, more free, more progressive, more generous, more philanthropic, more daring, courageous, lion-hearted than our forefathers, we have defaulted in our interest. And defaulters are always cowards if nothing worse. Let us not be cowards.

In California there are strong movements against the Japanese and the Chinese. It is easy to join the popular side, but it takes strength of heart and courage of mind and body sometimes to stand on the other side. I want to radiate my firm and unshakable conviction of the truth of human brotherhood, regardless of color, nationality, prejudice, or selfish and personal interest. Though the Japanese and Chinese, in open and honest business competition, take away my work, even then I want to radiate my firm belief in the *universal* brotherhood of man. And I want to do it without hesitation, as well as without fear. Hesitation too often means temporizing, evasion, shuffling, and I do not want to place myself open to any temptation to these things. Hence I would be prompt and outspoken in my adherence and advocacy of the fundamental principles of human brotherhood regardless of personal consequences and indifferent alike to praise or blame.

I believe in human democracy, in human freedom, in the equality of men and women; in morality, government, and household control; in resisting all tyrannies, whether of law, medicine, theology, or society; in the uplift of all the criminal and downtrodden; in the fair division of the profits of all labor; in the jealous preservation of the independence of every man and every woman; in the right of every child to be well born and welcomed, and of every woman to determine, without dictation from any one, whether she shall bear a child or not; in the abolition of all war; in the disarmament of all nations; in the abolition of land monopoly; in submitting every question to the test—the greatest possible good to the greatest number. These, as I now recall them, are the cardinal principles of my belief, my adherence to which I would fearlessly, without hesitation or equivocation, ever and always radiate.

CHAPTER XVI

RADIANCIES OF CONTENT AND DISCONTENT

I want to radiate a spirit of content. The dictionary says that to be content is to be "held full." If one is full, that is enough. He is satisfied. He has peace of mind. All this is implied in the word content. I want to radiate this sense of fullness, of satisfaction. I want people to feel that I am full of physical health, full of mental vigor, full of spiritual power, and, with the exceptions that I shall note later on in this chapter, that I am satisfied.

I want to radiate a large-hearted contentment with things as they are. I am content with the world as it is. Its glories, its beauties, its charms, its allurements, its variety, satisfy me. There is nothing in scenery that the mind can conceive that I cannot find; every sort of climate is offered to me. I can surround myself with people or I can dwell in the virgin solitudes. I can live under the gray skies of the East or under the cerulean blue of the West. The snow-covered heights of the Himalayas are mine or the wastes of the Sahara. I can toss on the stormy ocean or bask in the sun-kissed gardens of the South. It is a glorious, beautiful, blessed world.

Yet I hear people complaining on every hand. It is too hot, or they wish it hadn't rained. Why does the wind blow so fiercely? The snow has just come at the wrong time. Then, too, they find fault with the every-day occurrences of life. They are angry because they missed a train, have failed to carry through a business transaction, were delayed and lost an important appointment. The other day I met a young man holding his wrist, and with a look of severe pain on his face. In doing some work in the gymnasium he hurt his hand and wrist. It is hard to radiate contentment under the annoyance and pain of such things as this and the circumstances I have mentioned. Yet in these, as in all other things in life, I believe with Shakspeare:

> There is a Divinity that shapes our ends,
> Rough hew them as we may.

Many a time it is the best thing in the world to have lost an appointment, to have missed a train, to have sprained one's wrist. The wet weather is as good as the sunshine, and the storm equally beneficent with the calm. Hence I want to be content and to radiate my content with things as they are. Discontent is a burning acid. It eats away the happy, blessed things of life. It destroys the beauty of an otherwise perfect life. It takes away the smile and substitutes a frown. It injects bitterness into words that would otherwise be sweet. It changes the kind word into an angry curse. And it burns and corrodes far deeper than one imagines.

I once had a surgical operation in which a severe corroding substance was injected into a certain part of my body. My physicians, men of wisdom and men who loved me, thought they knew how much that corrosive substance would burn. But it burned far more severely and destroyed much more tissue than they conceived, and my life came near to paying the penalty. Discontent works in exactly the same way, only worse. Its burnings are of the mind, and, therefore, more seriously injurious. Its burns are deep and uncertain. To put it in another way—it sours the milk of human kindness. It turns the butter rancid. It pulls down the shades and shuts out the sunlight. It turns the steam off from the radiator. It shuts out the fresh air. It banishes the fairies of jollity, healthfulness, happiness, and content.

Do not radiate discontent, therefore, but radiate a glorious, buoyant, exuberant contentment. Think of the books we have to-day, as compared with those possessed by people who lived a few hundred years ago—the poems, the dramas, the essays, the histories, the novels, the accounts of adventure and travel, the revelations of science. Think how cheap they are, how easy to obtain. Think of the public libraries established in almost every city, town, and village of the civilized world. In many states they have now established a method by means of which the library systems may become county-wide in their influences instead of confined to the cities and towns. Books are being sent to the remotest farmhouse, to the shack of the lumberman, the moving home of the sheep-herder, the log hut of the miner, anywhere, everywhere that a human hand is seen stretched forth for a book, the new library system seeks to reach.

Think of the music of to-day! The great bands, the marvelous orchestras, the soul-inspiring choruses, the wonderfully equipped opera companies, the cheapness of the organ and piano, the universality of the graphophone, with its records of music of every character that can be heard in the humblest home.

Think of the multiplication of the opportunities for hearing the drama, some good, some indifferent, some bad, but all more or less revealing artistic power and calling forth the satisfaction of the onlookers.

Think of the spread of educational opportunities, the public schools, the colleges, the universities, the correspondence schools, the women's clubs and leagues. I went through a high school the other day that was ten times better equipped for the higher education, as far as it went, than the universities were a hundred years ago.

Think of the ease with which we travel—electric cars, railway trains, automobiles, flying machines.

Think of the annihilation of distance in conversing with our friends, the telephone, the telegraph, the telepost, the wireless.

Think of the opportunities of enjoyment and education offered to the poor in our large cities by means of the parks, the children's playgrounds, the free museums, and the art galleries.

Think of the improvements during late years in the conditions of home life —the application of gas and electricity for lighting, heating, cooking, ironing, and, now, even for sweeping and cleaning up.

Think of the improvements of the condition of lives of our farmers and their laborers in the remote districts. Little by little the conditions of life are being made easier for them. Labor is being lightened and the hours shortened, uncertainties are being eliminated, results made more sure.

Think of the growing spirit of freedom and true democracy, of brotherhood and comradeship that are welding the world together in the bonds of humanitarian brotherhood; treaties between nations, federations of nations, world's fairs, the Red Cross movement, The Hague Peace Tribunal, arbitration instead of war, and agitation for the reduction of armies and navies.[D]

One has but to study the changes that have taken place in our civilization since Dickens began to write, for instance, to see how wonderfully the world has progressed. He wrote *Nicholas Nickleby* to call attention to the horrible abuses existent in boys' boarding schools, where boys, who for any reason were desired out of the way at home, were put in charge of human fiends in the guise of "schoolmasters." Step-children, heirs who were in the way, natural children, and those whose parents had no natural affection for them, were put into these dens, and so cruelly abused that they often died; and at the best they dragged out their miserable existence afraid of what each hour of the day might bring forth and finding only in their troubled sleep the relief from the active cruelties they were made to bear.

Little Dorrit graphically pictured the horrors of the "prison for debt" system, and in the wonderfully painted character of Little Dorrit's father, Dickens showed how every human trait and feeling, every noble passion and emotion was dwarfed, twisted, distorted, and perverted by the action of this unnatural, cruel, and monstrous law.

Barnaby Rudge called equally vivid attention to the laws which placed political disabilities upon Jews and Roman Catholics, rendering them incapable of voting and holding office throughout the British dominions, and sought to remove the hatred, prejudice, and dissensions which unnatural acts of Parliament always caused.

In *A Tale of Two Cities* the curse of caste is revealed; the inevitable results of giving special privileges to a so-called aristocratic class, and while its teachings were veiled as being connected with incidents in the French Revolution they were a wonderful help to the forwarding of true ideas of pure democracy and genuine recognition of the doctrine of the brotherhood of man.

In *Martin Chuzzlewit* the theme is the horrors of the "Circumlocution Office"—that vast, hideous, monstrous juggernaut that rode rough-shod over all justice, truth, honor, right, decency, and sincerity, by its evasions, quibblings, dodgings, twinings, twistings, and deliberate perversions of the truth.

Other writers made their novels the themes of similar crying abuses that needed reform. Henry Cockton wrote his *Valentine Vox the Ventriloquist* to expose the hideous dealings of private mad-houses, where helpless men and women were confined by law, who were perfectly sane, yet who were in the way of dishonest lawyers, judges, administrators, heirs, or relations. I can never forget the powerful and terrible impression this story made upon me, though it is nearly forty years since I read it, especially where the author described what it is said he himself had had to pass through, when he was driven into temporary insanity by being strapped to his cot while fiends in human form mocked and taunted him and at the same time "tickled his feet" until he was a raging maniac.

To the people of to-day the term "Chartist" means nothing. Nine-tenths of the population of the United States possibly never heard the term. Yet it is only a few generations since men were sentenced to "Botany Bay" and other penal settlements for twenty, thirty, and more years, and sometimes "for life," for joining in this reform which demanded certain rights that *we* have enjoyed without a thought ever since we were born. One of these grand old warriors for man's greater freedom used to visit at my father's house when I was a lad. He was an intellectual giant who had won the honor and fame the world freely accords to those who do not take it by the throat too severely, and once in a while he could be induced to tell of the days of his earlier conflict;—how that he and his compeers fought for a repeal of the corn laws—laws which made it almost impossible for a poor man to get bread—and for the right of a man to sell the products of his own labor from door to door to save himself from starvation. He was imprisoned and sentenced for a long term of years and while in prison wrote a poem of tremendous power and influence. How my heart burned to the old warrior, and I then and there declared that

> I live to learn their story
>   Who've suffered for my sake,
> To emulate their glory,
>   And to follow in their wake:

> For the cause that lacks assistance,
> For the wrong that needs resistance.

Then, too, how I recall the fight for religious freedom in England—some of it before my time, but some of it under my own eyes, and in which I had the joy of bearing a small part. The Lord George Gordon riots, described by

Dickens in *Barnaby Rudge,* were provoked by religious hostility. When I was a boy, no Jew or Catholic could hold office in England—I think I am correct. This act, passed in the reign of Charles II—I write from memory—was thus in operation for two hundred years; two hundred years of injustice, prejudice, fostering of religious hatred and separations. Yet Benjamin Disraeli made a great premier, and was one of the most brilliant statesmen of Europe, and the Howard family, Cardinal Manning, and Cardinal Newman, all of whom were Roman Catholics, were loved and revered on every hand for their enlightened patriotism and the help they gave to everything that had the welfare of England at heart. It was a glad day for England that saw the removal of the disabilities from such good citizens as these, merely because they chose to exercise their perfect God-given right of freedom of choice in religious belief. And still, even as late as the ascension to the throne of George V, son of King Edward, and grandson of that progressive and liberal-minded Queen, Victoria, there remained in the oath a hateful spirit of narrowness and intolerance against Catholic beliefs. Thirty to forty years previously Charles Bradlaugh was refused his seat in the House of Commons because he desired to "affirm" instead of "taking the oath." He was an "unbeliever," and claimed his right to be such, and yet to take his seat as a representative of the people without being compelled to swear to an oath in which he did not believe. He was fought an every hand, and with physical violence; yet he kept resolutely on with the conflict, until I saw him myself, with joy, take his place before the speaker of the House, victorious. Yet I am not an unbeliever, nor do I accept Bradlaugh's conclusions as to God and the making of the universe. Nor is it necessary. Equally so it is not necessary that I should attempt to force my ideas down his throat and if he refuse to say that he swallows them should seek to keep him from exercising his political rights.

To us, living to-day, it seems impossible that a great civil war was necessary ere the shackles were shaken from the limbs of four millions of slaves; it seems incredible that New Englanders as well as Southerners were engaged in fostering the iniquitous slave trade—the murderous trade in human flesh and blood. Grant everything the South claims to-day as to the difficulty of handling the negro problem, that does not alter the fundamental principle of the Declaration of Independence that "all men are created equal; that they are endowed by their Creator with certain inalienable rights; that among these are life, liberty, and the pursuit of happiness." To us it seems incredible that honest and honorable men, clear-sighted, clear-brained religious men who knew the value of words and their meaning, could have so befuddled their intellects, let alone their moral nature, as to dare to read these words and at the same time own slaves. Yet it was so, and not until the heroes whose work led ultimately to the Declaration of Independence for the slave, called the Emancipation Proclamation, set their faces against this great iniquity, was anything done to mitigate its evils.

How well do I recall the endeavors of many Englishmen to induce the Government to interfere with the Turks and prevent further infliction of horrible and murderous atrocities upon the Bulgarians and other subject people, because of religious differences. But "politics stood in the way." And yet I heard the words of Cleveland ring around the world when he bade England: "Hands off," from Venezuela. Again was I thrilled when McKinley justified the prophecy of Joaquin Miller, uttered nearly thirty years previously, in his *Cuba Libre*, where he declared:

> She shall rise, by all that's holy!
> She shall live and she shall last;

> She shall rise as rose Columbus,
> From his chains, from shame and wrong—
> Rise as Morning, matchless, wondrous—
>
> Rise as some rich morning song—
> Rise a ringing song, and story,
> Valor, Love personified.
> Stars and stripes espouse her glory,
> Love and Liberty allied.

The time came when we "flashed her lights of freedom," as we had done before, but this time there was an admixture of personal feeling in which the cry, "Remember the *Maine*," bore a large part. Yet the main issue was raised, viz., the intervention of a strong power to prevent another strong power from too seriously oppressing a confessedly weak power. This is a step in the right direction. The bully, whether in school, in the street, in business, or among nations, should be taught that his bullying is unsafe, and that if he must fight he must choose a "fellow of his own size."

While I do not close my eyes to the facts that nations are human and liable to err, I hail this as a great forward step, and was filled with rejoicing when the United States Government refused to accept any indemnity from China for its share of the expense of putting down the last great Boxer Rebellion.

In our National and State governments there is a growing spirit of righteous intervention. In his last presidential message, President Taft voiced this spirit in his recommendation of an enlarged measure of protection for railroad employees, and states and cities are moving more rapidly than ever before in the enactment of laws and ordinances for the protection of those least able to protect themselves.

Reforms in law procedure are progressing. In his 1910 message, President Taft thus spoke:

> One great crying need in the United States is cheapening the cost of litigation by simplifying judicial procedure and expediting final judgment. Under present conditions the poor man is at a woeful disadvantage in a legal contest with a corporation or a rich opponent. The necessity for this reform exists both in United States courts and in all state courts. In order to bring it about, however, it naturally falls to the general government by its example to furnish a model to all States.

This is a great step in the right direction. The honest and manly recognition of a crying evil is often the beginning of its removal, and I sincerely hope to live to see the day when our laws, and legislative procedure, will truthfully be equally for the poor and the rich.

The activity of the Federal Government in pursuing the nefarious malefactors who are conducting the "white slave traffic," is also a sign of marked improvement in affording protection to those who are helpless and often unable and incompetent to know what to do for their own welfare.

And how I hail with joy the movement so energetically furthered by Mr. Bok, of the *Ladies' Home Journal*, the Bishop of London, the *Physical Culture* magazine, *Collier's*, and others, for the education of the young of both sexes as to the sacred relations of sex and all they imply. The W. C. T. U. has done a little, the magazines and physical culture movement more, and now the better schools—such as the Polytechnic High School of Los Angeles, and the High School in Pasadena, California—are giving definite and specific instruction upon these matters to boys and girls whose parents have been remiss in neglecting this all-important part of their *home* education and training.

The pure food bill is another step forward in our national progress; the great conservation movement and the work of the United States Reclamation Service, which is providing means for irrigating the soil and thus rendering possible the establishment of thousands of homes on lands that otherwise would be arid and useless—these are gigantic strides of advancement. The postal-savings bank and parcels post are already facts, thus demonstrating that, little by little, the powers that have controlled our Government, for the benefit of the few, instead of for all the people, and especially those who need such benefit the most, are gradually losing their hold. Soon, let us hope, we shall have the "penny postage"—one cent for a letter instead of two, as now. The extension of the eight-hour day law; the honest endeavors now being made to give labor a fair opportunity to state its needs and requirements and thus help bring oppressive employers to time, are also forward steps. Granted that labor often makes unreasonable and unjust demands, let it not be forgotten that it is only within the last few decades that they have been allowed to have a voice at all. For centuries they have been "chained to the wheel of labor,"

> The emptiness of ages in their face,
> And on their back the burden of the world.

What if, now that "whirlwinds of rebellion" are shaking the world and these hitherto "dumb terrors" have found, or are finding, a voice, they speak a little too loudly, or too harshly, or ask more than they ought? Whose fault is it? Who has kept them in bondage so long? They will learn, by and by, to speak more rationally, but this will come only by speaking, so I hail with delight the fact that "the rulers and lords of all lands" are recognizing their right to be heard, and are more or less respectfully listening to what they have to say.

It is another grand sign of universal progress that the owners and landlords of vile tenement houses, of the horrible kennels in which human beings in the past used to be penned as in pigsties, are no longer allowed to reap monetary rewards from such abominable and cursed holes. Boards of health, civic improvement bodies, tenement reform associations are taking upon themselves the work of protecting the poor, helpless, and often unfortunate dwellers in these plague spots and compelling that they be made decent, healthful, and sanitary—often seeing that they are razed and entirely removed. What though oftentimes the people who dwell in these places are brought thither by their own misconduct? Are men, women, and innocent children to be "damned" on this earth—as well as in the future—because morally they have been weak and unfortunate? The greater the weakness and the lower the fall, the greater the cry and need for help. Jacob Riis was a brave and heroic leader in New York, William Booth and his gallant army in London and the thousand and one other cities of the world, and the day is dawning when there will be no "slums" in any decent, self-respecting city, when such books as *How the Other Half Lives*, *The Submerged Tenth*, *If Christ Came to Chicago*, and *The People of the Abyss* can no longer be written, for the true-hearted, loving, brotherly, and sisterly, will have been aroused to do their plain, simple, and manifest duty and "slums," "abysses," and "plague spots" will cease to exist.

There are many other excellent things I might comment upon that help bring content to the soul. They betoken a glorious and blessed improvement upon the "days of things as they were" and they should lead every man to get into line, to find the step and keep it, marching on with this vanguard of human progress, which seeks the best possible condition of body, mind, and soul for all men.

Yet, in spite of this large-hearted contentment with things as they are, and with the way the world generally is progressing, which I would radiate, I would equally radiate a great discontent with many things as they are. When I look at my own faults and failings, my inadequacies and incompetencies, my blindness and stupidity, my ignorance and willfulness, I find much of my content disappear like the airy visions of a dream. I certainly do not want to be content with these things and so I call up as often as I can a mighty discontent which is a constant urge to the higher, nobler, truer, better life. I am as self-willed as other men, and yet I well know that human will is both ignorant and blind, and that only when it is made subject to the Great Controlling Will of the Universe will it lead me aright and in the paths of ultimate, permanent success. And by success, I do not mean the paltry thing most men regard as success. I certainly wish to radiate discontent with what men generally regard as success. Mere money, fame, honor, social distinction, count for little unless character, divine sympathy with one's needy fellows, and an enlarged conception of the brotherhood of men accompany them.

And how can I do other than radiate a large and tremendous discontent at the suffering and woe of the unfortunates of life? It is little or nothing to me what causes their misfortune. I have learned that the judgment of sociologists, theologians, and reformers generally is of little account in interpreting the causes of things. As a rule, they look only on the surface and see nothing of the hidden springs of action and therefore know little of the movement of hearts of men and women whose condition they so complacently and conceitedly imagine they can change.

Some years ago, Jack London wrote a book entitled, *The People of the Abyss*. It was severely censured and criticised and some critics went so far as to assert that it was full of untruths. It told of the dismal lives of London's poor, who daily find themselves with nothing but one meal, two meals, three meals between themselves and starvation—poor wretches to whom the "wolf at the door" is an ever present reality, and who tremble every time their employers look towards them with a frown or speak with a voice that threatens dismissal. What a frightful, pitiable, pathetic position for men and women—my brothers and sisters—to be in. I certainly do not wish to radiate contentment at the fact of their unfortunate condition. I want somehow to take some of their burdens upon my life. I want to realize something of the spirit that led Walt Whitman to exclaim, "I will take nothing for myself that cannot be given upon equal terms to all men."

When I read the stories of child labor and learn of the many cruelties practiced upon helpless little ones, in the name of business; when I see those boys and girls of tender age in the cotton mills of the South, owned by wealthy men of the North, plodding back and forth, hour by hour, behind the whirling spindles; when I see them, as I have often done, so utterly weary that when the noon hour came, they would stretch out on the bare floor and try to gain a little snatch of forgetfulness of their weariness in sleep, rather than eat their inadequate lunch, I have certainly felt, as I now feel, that I wish to radiate a tremendous amount of discontent that such inhuman facts can exist. When I see the private palace car owned by the many-times millionaire, and catch glimpses of the extravagant and wasteful luxury in which he and his family live, and realize that this prodigal wastefulness is made possible by the life-destroying labor of poor, anæmic children in the glass-blowing factories of New Jersey, I wish I had the power to send a great wail of discontent through the country that would thrill the hearts, awaken the senses, and arouse the consciences of every man and woman in the nation.

When I realize the inadequacies of our legal system to do justice alike to all men and women, the poor as well as the rich, the innocent and confiding as well as the crafty and cunning, I feel nothing but discontent and long for the time to come when justice and mercy shall be of higher value in the courts of our land than precedent and legal procedure.

It often takes moral courage to radiate real living discontent with these injustices and crimes against our needy and defenseless fellows. I long to possess this moral courage in fullest measure, and to radiate it on every hand. In view of the need for strong protest against the smug, contented betrayers of the poor and needy, I would radiate a spirit that has not inaptly been termed that of *contemporaneous protest and rebellion.* By this I mean that present spirit of protest and rebellion against wrongs that exist *now*, so that my protest will be contemporaneous with the evil.

It is easy enough to line up with the winning side and shout Hurrah! with the victors in any conflict. Even the English of to-day agree that the American Revolution was a good thing and that the acts of George III were indefensible tyranny. But it required considerable courage to join one's forces with those of Washington when money was scarce and men few, when the day seemed dark and gloomy, and the prospects of success were doubtful.

It is easy enough to-day to Hurrah! for the principles of Lincoln, but many a great statesman like Henry Clay felt it was better to compromise than face the fierce antagonism of such men as Calhoun, Jefferson Davis, and others who believed in the opposing ideas.

What I desire with all my heart is to radiate not only my *readiness* and *willingness* to line up with the unpopular cause, *but the fact that I am already lined up*. That, without being asked, people will know what my position is sure to be; that I naturally belong on the side of the "under dog," and that in any conflict against entrenched power and wrong, where the weak and oppressed are fighting for rights which are inherently theirs, that as soon as I hear the battle-cry my "Here!" will ring out immediate, bold and clear.

Nor do I always want to wait to be called upon. I may not have either the wisdom and discretion or the ability to be a leader and I have no desire to thrust myself forward as such. At the same time, I do not want to be cowardly and hang back when I see that which I feel is inherently wrong. Even though I stand alone, I want to stand in protest and contemporaneous rebellion against the wrong that I see.

Nay, further, I want to radiate as *my habitual attitude of mind* that I am ever on the alert to *seek out opportunities for rebellion* against any and all systems of wrong, no matter how powerful, that I may gladly take upon my shoulders some part of the burden of helping forward the real progress of the entire human race.

James Russell Lowell expressed the passionate desire of my heart in his *Present Crisis*. In that majestic poem he shows the need for this contemporaneous rebellion:

> Backward look across the ages, and the beacon-movements see,
> That, like peaks of some sunk continent, jut through Oblivion's Sea;
> Not an ear in court or market for the low foreboding cry
> Of those Crises, God's stern winnowers, from whose feet Earth's chaff must fly;
> Never shows the choice momentous till the judgment hath passed by.
> Careless seems the great Avenger; history's pages but record
> One death-grapple in the darkness 'twixt old systems and the Word;
> Truth forever on the scaffold, wrong forever on the throne,—
> Yet that scaffold sways the future, and behind the dim unknown
> Standeth God within the shadow, keeping watch above His own.

The whole poem is full of this passionate great-hearted, manly, God-like sympathy, *now* and *here*, with the needy, the oppressed, the helpless of today. The crises are here now, those stern winnowers that test and try men's souls, that discover whether they are wheat or chaff, ashes or gold. Oh, for men who have made already the "choice momentous"—while the battle is raging, when there is danger, risk, peril, possible death in the conflict. Is he a true man who waits, pauses, hesitates, wavers in such conflicts, "till the judgment hath passed by"?

I would radiate, again let me say it, my readiness to march at the sound of the drum, to advance with the front ranks, to fight at the first word.

History affords us many noble examples and "beacon lights" of those who have lived in accordance with the principles herein laid down.

Stephen Langton and the barons of England protested against the tyrannical power of King John. They did so at the peril of their heads. Yet they were possessed of this spirit of contemporaneous rebellion, and they fought against John and won from him that great charter of the liberties of men, that has been the basis of all proclamations of freedom ever since.

Cromwell, Hampden, Pym, Milton, and the other great commoners and democrats of England were in a state of contemporaneous protest and rebellion against the undue pretensions of King Charles I. Their protests might have cost them their lives—yet they protested. And they won a victory that has made republics possible throughout all time.

So with the leaders of the French Revolution. There were many awful and bloody events connected with that great act of contemporaneous protest, but that the ultimate outcome upon mankind has been good most true-hearted thinkers agree. Yet the protests were made by the earlier agitators under great danger.

When Patrick Henry, Franklin, Jefferson, Adams, Washington, and the other American revolutionists protested against King George's tyranny, and when the noble band met at Philadelphia and signed the Declaration of Independence, they knew they did it at the peril of their lives—yet they protested and won for mankind the victory that Joaquin Miller calls "Time's burst of Dawn."

Had Langton, Cromwell, the French Revolutionists, Washington, and the signers of the Declaration of Independence failed, they would all have forfeited their lives for their temerity. It was an act of great moral courage to rebel.

When Galileo rebelled against the dictum of the ecclesiastic authorities in regard to the movement of the earth, it meant his imprisonment, yet he rebelled and thus ushered in a new day of advancement in astronomical knowledge. Darwin did the same. Both men required daring and courage, yet they did not hesitate or falter.

There are evils to-day that should be fought; fashions, customs, entrenched wrongs in existence *now* against which manly men are called to be in contemporaneous rebellion. Those of us who live to-day are reaping great and blessed privileges, freedom, liberties, won for us as the result of the protests, rebellions, warfares of the moral heroes of the past; so should we further the progress of the world by protesting and fighting the existing wrongs, in order that future generations may be freer than we are, and may push on still further the glorious chariot of human progress.

Henry George was a recent heroic example of contemporaneous protest against current evils. Garibaldi, Mazzini, Victor Hugo, Kossuth, were all noble and inspiring examples of the like spirit. Ruskin's life was a perpetual protest against the sacrificing of beauty, peace, harmony, and brotherhood for the rush and show of material prosperity. William Morris's life, work, voice, and pen were ever in active, open, contemporaneous hostility and opposition to the damnable spirit of modern competition, and demoralizing commercialism which destroyed artistic labor, banished fellowship, and substituted therefor the rule of the jungle where the strong devour the weak. Thank God! the ranks of the morally courageous have always found glad and willing recruits; men willing to spend and be spent for the benefit of humanity; willing to be rebels and accounted and treated as such that they might help gain larger victories of freedom for their fellow-men.

We sometimes think that there was more moral heroism in the days gone by than there is to-day. I do not believe it! In this matter of moral heroism and contemporaneous rebellion against entrenched wrong, we have many fine and noble living examples on every hand. I could mention a hundred of them in as many minutes. A few must suffice.

When Edwin Markham wrote *The Man with the Hoe*, he showed his spirit of contemporaneous protest and rebellion. Here was no reflection upon labor or its dignity, as some thoughtless critics have affirmed, but it was a tremendous and powerful onslaught upon the "Kings and Rulers of All Lands" who permit employers to chain the laborer to the "wheel of labor." Markham's poem is a direct challenge and throwing down of the gauntlet to those who contend that they have a right to purchase labor in the open market at any price, however demoralizing to mankind. It is a contention that manhood is more than money; that the laborer is more than the labor; and that the employers who value the labor done more than the men who do the labor are unworthy the honor and respect of decent men; are unworthy to be called real men because of their tyrannical abuse of their helpless brothers.

William Booth, president of the Salvation Army, Jack London, the socialist novelist, Jacob Riis, the New York newspaper idealist, Maud Ballington Booth, the leader of the Volunteers of America, Charles Montgomery, of San Francisco, the prisoner's friend, and Dana Bartlett, of Los Angeles, the brother of poor "Dagoes," Portuguese and Mexicans, are all more or less widely diverse examples of contemporaneous rebellion and protest against existing social conditions. Each works in his own way to ameliorate these conditions, but the work of each is a protest against those laws of supply and demand, of competition, of worship of material things, that allow it to be possible that some men can gain more wealth than they can ever utilize, even if they lived to be ten thousand years old, and never earn another cent, whilst others can earn barely enough to keep body and soul together and who live every day in dread of the future because they are capable of earning no more than enough to keep them one, two, or three meals away from starvation.

In a copy of his book, *The People of the Abyss*, which Jack London sent to me, which truthfully portrays the life of the submerged tenth of London, he wrote something like this on the title page: "Dear James—With the facts of these pages before me, I may agree with you in your favorite quotation from Browning, that 'God's in his heaven,' but I cannot agree with you that 'All's right with the world.'"

It is the fashion with certain people to decry Jack London's socialism, but I happen to know that he has personally sacrificed thousands of dollars to his principles in this matter, has lost the friendship of many wealthy people who would have showered their gifts upon him had he been complacent towards what he calls "predatory wealth," hence I hail his acts of contemporaneous rebellion and his taking upon himself of the battle for these, his weaker brothers and sisters, as heroic, and fully worthy of the highest esteem of all good men, whatever they may think of the methods by which he would bring about the desired changes.

All through his life there has been a strong current of contemporaneous rebellion and belligerent sincerity in the work of the poet of the Sierras, Joaquin Miller. He was brought up as a Quaker and taught to believe in non-resistance, hence he preached peace at the beginning of the Civil War until his printing office was wrecked and his life threatened. When the world at large was condemning the Indian, he went and stood by his side, and when he believed him to be in the right, fought battles on his behalf. All through his life he has boldly stood for man's larger freedom, and against entrenched tyranny. When England made war upon the Boers, he denounced the warlike and jingo politicians with a power and strength seldom surpassed in poetry, in spite of the fact that the English had always been his best friends and the largest purchasers of his poems.

While he lived in California, not far from San Francisco, and California was a hotbed of the sentiment that demands the exclusion of the Chinese and Japanese, he ever fearlessly and in unmistakable terms denounced this action as opposed to the fundamental principles of the fatherhood of God and the brotherhood of man, and demanded of his fellow citizens that they adhere strictly to these never-failing and abiding truths.

These men are but few of the many I might mention, but they will serve as types. They have been and are willing to suffer for the general good of mankind. Therefore, in the presence of their moral heroism and courage, let us cry with George Linnæus Banks:

>   I live to learn their story
>   Who've suffered for my sake,
>   To emulate their glory,
>   And to follow in their wake;
>   Bards, patriots, martyrs, sages,
>   The noble of all ages,

Whose deeds crowd history's pages
   And Time's great volume make.

I live ...
For the cause that lacks assistance,
For the wrong that needs resistance,
For the future in the distance,
   And the good that I can do.

CHAPTER XVII

RADIANCIES OF SINCERITY

We need more of the virtue of belligerent sincerity. What the world needs to-day is bold, outspokenness for principle. It is not enough that we hold principles in the quietude of our own homes and discuss them in the sanctity of our bedrooms. We need a belligerent sincerity of fundamental principles in the mart, the store, in the counting house, in the bank, on the board of trade, and the stock exchange. The tendency of men in office and men in employment is to be subservient for the purpose of their own advancement. It is so easy to yield a principle to gain an increase in salary or to win the support of a swaying party vote. In this age of great aggregations of capital, when corporations are conducting gigantic enterprises, it is so easy for subordinates to place all the responsibility of conscience upon their chiefs and to refuse to accept responsibility for acts of which they themselves are the instruments on the plea, "I am but a servant and carry out the will of my superior." Relentless crushing out of competitors, secretly securing rebates, unjust discrimination in discounts, the utilization of official information for personal advantage or that of one's friends, the writing of editorials contrary to one's principles because the policies of the paper require it, in other words, the whole realm of truckling subserviency, yielding, cowardice, obsequiousness, surrender, fawning, servility, sycophancy, toad-eating, pliancy, should be weeded out of the garden of the soul and belligerent sincerity planted in their stead.

At the same time, I want to radiate my abhorrence of all the truckling subserviency that seeks to gain its ends and make secure its own position by cringing, fawning, and flattery upon those whose favor it seeks.

Most men have their pet vanities. Few are free from weaknesses and frailties. It is so easy to flatter, so natural to "kow-tow," so profitable to pander. The reason that the world so laughs at the delineations of the open, bold, corrupt, parasitical, pandering Falstaff is that they find the echo in their own meannesses of soul. Like Henry VII, many men have their Falstaffs, who seek to eat, drink, and be merry at their expense.

By this I do not mean to decry and impeach the integrity and sincerity of those who express sympathy and appreciation of those who are engaged in large enterprises. It is natural for those conducting such to seek and require such sympathy in their lieutenants, but to such lieutenants I would cry mightily and constantly, "Sympathize and commend by all means, but when you do, be sure your purest virtue is on guard over your heart and your lips. Say nothing that you do not absolutely mean." Be "belligerently sincere" with your own soul and speak no words to your employer because he enjoys them that you would not *as freely and gladly say if he had dismissed you from his employ.*

I would also radiate my appreciation of those who, occupying what we call a subordinate position, speak out with frank, plain, direct simplicity the thoughts of their hearts. I have sometimes found in business, employers who sought by undue flattery, scheming, plotting, chicanery, and fraud, all stealthily exercised, to "work" their employees and secure from them a meed of service for which they were not willing to pay a full and just price. In dealing with such employers a frank, open, simple-hearted, and honest employee is often at a great disadvantage. Being used to tortuous, underground, secret, plotting methods himself, such an employer regards with suspicion the simple actions of his employee. He sees in his frank openness nothing but deeply laid plots. He finds in his candid sincerity craftily planned schemes. The more open the one, the more certain the other is that there is something hidden, deep, far-reaching, cunning, and deceitful underneath his acts.

To these open-hearted souls I would radiate a tonic that is stimulating—quickening to their moral fiber and stiffening and strengthening to their moral spines. To such I would come as a cold shower bath to stimulate the nerves and muscles to greater tension. Stand by your truthfulness, stand by your frankness, stand by your openness until you teach these burrowing, crafty, stealthy, sly, evasive, sneaking creatures that openness is better than secrecy, light better than darkness, truth better than falsity, candor better than craft, and an open enemy better than a secret, fawning, sycophantic foe.

CHAPTER XVIII

RADIANCIES OF SERVICE

I want to radiate by thought, word, and act the joy and blessedness of service. What a privilege it is to be able to do something for your fellows! How great and constant is the joy of ministering! How ready we are to run with willing feet to do some little or big thing for those we love! The lover will climb dangerous Alpine heights to get the rare and richly treasured edelweiss for his beloved. Leander gladly and joyously braved the dangers of the Hellespont that he might cheer and encourage his Hero. The lover has always cried, in all ages, to his loved one, asking her to send him on some difficult errand. He would gladly go anywhere, to any service, however arduous and dangerous, to prove his love. The records of chivalry are full of daring deeds accomplished by men in order to please the women they loved.

Against this kind of service I have nothing to say. At the same time, this is not the kind of service of which I now write. I would radiate the thought that in our service we should treat all men and women with the same willing gladness of ministry that the lover has for the mistress of his heart. I desire to be ready and willing to fly on the wings of helpfulness to do service for the meanest and most despicable of human kind, if thereby he, or she, may be benefited. I would radiate the belief that our willing service belongs to humanity, all men, all women, not to a select few, not to the small and chosen circle whom we call our loved ones and friends. I would radiate the spirit of service that possessed and animated the strong, pure soul of William Morris, that led him to place his precious time and service at the disposal of a committee of men, not one of whom knew enough to appreciate his exquisite and beautiful devotion, and under whose control he was ready to go and speak words of cheer, fellowship, and brotherhood in the lowest and most degraded parts of London. He was imbued with this passion for service and it was service to the whole of mankind—not the chosen few.

I once picked up some socialistic newspaper with which I was not familiar, but in it was an account of the life of a man who had recently died. According to the story of his biographer, this man was carried away with this passion for human service to the lowest and most degraded, and he had spent his active and busy life in ministering to those who, as a rule, are ignored by their more fortunate brothers and sisters. It was a story that thrilled me to a higher and nobler endeavor.

Many a time I have bowed my soul in reverence and humility before a group of Salvation Army lasses who, with sweet, gentle ministrations, have cheered the dwellers in the wretched hovels of London, New York, and other cities. I know one maiden, delicately constituted, and reared in a home full of wealth and luxury, who felt this passionate call of service so strongly, that, in spite of the protests of her relatives and friends, she went to London, united with the Salvation Army, and with her own beautiful and gentle hands, down upon her knees, has scrubbed into cleanliness the floor of a drunken wife and drunken husband whose children had never known a clean floor in the whole of their dirty and wretched lives. I have helped her clean out the accumulated filth, of what seemed to be months, in similar wretched places, and all this, as well as the more refined ministrations of the mind and soul, were offered with a sweet and gentle insistence that no one could take offense at, and without an air of conscious self-approbation that one so often finds in those who are seeking to minister to others.

But it is not only in this larger and devoted sense that I would radiate my desire to serve and minister to my fellows. It is in the small and every-day things of life, no matter what my work or surroundings may be, that I would radiate this ministering spirit. What a pleasure it is to do things for others. What a joy to realize that your friends love you enough to want you to do something for them.

I find, however, that in the mind of many is the idea that certain service is menial, and that they would not serve if they were not obliged to do so for the money it brings. I have a deep and profound pity in my soul for those who look upon life with this perverted vision. If I were a waiter in a cheap restaurant, it seems to me it would be my joy to serve the cheap meals as quickly and as cheerfully as I possibly could. Surely ministering to the bodily wants of men and women is a service which ought to be blessed. If I were a housemaid I feel that I should find joy in making and keeping everything as orderly and tidy as possible.

I have several times stayed in a semi-public institution where a great number of nurses were employed, and I have watched both men and women engaged in this beautiful service. In this particular place they all seemed full of this passion for service. There was no impatience at the often exacting calls and demands of the querulous and unreasonable invalids. Their very lives were a dedication.

Sometimes we meet with those who will refuse to do certain things because they regard them as more menial than those they were engaged to perform, as, for instance, the case of a bell boy who refused to take away a coal-scuttle when asked to do so because that was not in the list of his duties, and a man "lower down in the scale" was supposed to attend to work of that kind. Now, while I recognize that there must be for convenience's sake, a division of labor, I want to radiate the feeling and belief that there is no higher, no lower, in this call of personal service. It is just as honorable to be a street sweeper or a scavenger of the meanest kind (so-called), to be a farm laborer, to be a kitchen drudge, to be a factory hand, as it is to be a minister of a church that pays a salary of $20,000 a year. The real blessedness of life of all grades of service from the scavenger to the expensive pastor is determined by the *spirit* behind the service, and the kitchen drudge who does her work with the consciousness in her own soul that she is gladly, merrily, cheerfully undertaking her work and doing it well for the comfort, benefit, cheer, and blessing of her employers is of more benefit to mankind than the services of the expensive pastor of the exclusive church who regards his ministry as a proof of his own intellectual worth, and as a means of asserting his high social position.

Who can ever forget the wonderful picture of that sturdy Scotch Doctor depicted by Ian Maclaren in his *Bonnie Brier Bush*, whose passion of devotion and ministry was so pure that it reached every soul in the whole region.

Frances Hodgson Burnett, in her *Dawn of a To-morrow*, tells of a degraded street waif who yet had this passion of ministry in her soul, and I have come to the conclusion that wherever it is found, it is divine, and therefore blessed. Hence I would radiate it at all times, under all conditions, and under all circumstances to all classes and conditions of men.

Where would have been the work of Judge Lindsay of Denver, Golden Rule Jones of Toledo, McClaughery of Elmira Penitentiary, Chief Kohler of Cleveland, Governor Hunt and Warden Sims of Arizona, if they had worked only for the worthy? It was the very openness of the unworthiness of those for whom they strove, that made the appeal to these large-hearted men.

It is so easy to criticise men of this stamp because they have dared to break away from the conventional rendering of service only to the worthy. It is so easy to cry that they are doing more harm than good. But those who know the work and know the hearts that are constantly being touched and molded into betterment by it are better able to judge of its higher results.

Shall I hesitate to render service because I myself am not perfect? Shall I refuse to give the shivering and hungry beggar on the street a twenty-five cent meal ticket because I myself am not free from debt? Shall I refuse to guide the lost wayfarer because I myself do not know all the winding pathways of life?

By no means! Let me do the best I may while I may, and seize every opportunity that arises. It was a Christian minister that dared to rebuke Father Damien by claiming that he was not immaculate in his service to the repulsive and loathsome lepers of Molokai. And it was Robert Louis Stevenson who showed that Christian minister what true Christianity would have led him to say instead of what he did say. Father Damien's ministry was self-sacrificing, noble, and divine, even though,—granting for the moment the truth of the minister's slander,—his service was touched of the earth, earthy. Yet the beneficence and blessedness of it was so supremely above the smug, self-satisfied, standing-aloofness of the "immaculate" ministerial critic that Stevenson's colossal rebuke to the latter found perfect echo in the heart of every decent man and woman throughout the world. Joaquin Miller expresses the same thought in his beautiful and strong poem on Father Damien when he says:

Why do ye not as he has done?

If we can do so much better than those we criticise, why, in the name of heaven and suffering humanity, do we not go ahead and do it? Let us do our best regardless of our own infirmities and weakness and the consequent criticisms of others.

So I want to radiate to the needy and unworthy my readiness, nay, my anxiety to serve them whenever and wherever I possibly can. And though my service be not unmixed gold, though there be in it some of the dross of imperfection, I would not withhold my hand on that account, but I would serve the more readily and gladly in the hope and assurance that by suffering with the needy and unworthy in their need and unworthiness the fire of their pain and sorrow may help refine away the dross in me and leave only that of pure gold.

"Give to the needy! *worthy* or *unworthy*!" should be the battle cry of him who wishes to be a blessing to his fellows, and the more unworthy the needy are, the more loving and wise the service should be. When Walt Whitman was shedding blessing, benediction, comfort, and joy on every hand throughout the hospitals of Washington, he had little or no money to give. He asked no questions when he went to the bedside of the sick and dying soldier boys as to whether they were worthy or not. They were needy and that was enough for him. He stayed and soothed their weary hours by telling them stories, reading to them, writing letters home for them, and in a thousand and one little and big ways seeking to make their sick beds more tolerable during the long hours of enforced confinement.

One of his rules for the making of a true poet was that he should "give alms to all who ask," and that he should "stand up for the stupid and crazy." I have a friend in Chicago who seeks absolutely to live these two rules in his daily life. Even though he may often give to the unworthy, he feels he can better afford to do that than to miss once giving to a really needy person lest he might be giving to some one who was neither needy nor worthy.

A poet, whom I am very fond of quoting, once wrote:

> In men whom men condemn as ill,
> I find so much of goodness still;
> In men whom men account divine,
> I find so much of sin and blot;
> I hesitate to draw the line between the two;
> Where God has not.

It is impossible properly and wisely to differentiate, and because a man is unworthy is all the more reason that his fellows should seek to help him into a state of worthiness.

How I wish I could imbue all with the spirit that moves Charles Montgomery, the prisoner's friend of San Francisco. He goes to the state penitentiaries at San Quentin and Folsom, and arranges to give help to the prisoners as soon as they are released. Nay, he provides places for them and then goes before the board of parole and secures their release. He takes a true brother's interest in the men and seeks to win them to a nobler life. Doubtless he is often deceived, but in scores of cases he starts the men on the up-grade. What is one failure or ten, to one success or ten? If it were *my* son that was saved I should be most grateful even though he saved but one. It would make his work glorious and blessed to me. Then try to feel what it must be for some other father or mother to learn that his, or her, son is saved from the life of hell, to the life of heaven, here and now, and do as much for that son as you would for your own.

I doubt not that some of the boys Judge Lindsay seeks to save in Denver, are not all they ought to be, and that sometimes he is disappointed in the results. But does this make him lose heart, or cease to work for the new cases that come? By no means! It makes him more determined than ever to reach their hearts. He is more tender, more long-suffering, more patient, more sympathetic, more loving. The greater the need the greater the endeavor.

The other day I sat down to the dinner table with a friend who outlined to me a project in which himself and four others are interested. It is to buy a farm, on the shores of a small but beautiful lake, a few miles out from one of our great cities, and there establish a home and a school for needy children. These five devoted young people are now working hard and each one is saving every cent he can out of his own earnings that, without calling upon any one else, they may be able to buy the farm. I had asked my friend why he did not go to hear the great actress Bernhardt. The reason was that he preferred to put the three dollars that a ticket to hear Bernhardt would have cost into his "child farm fund." Here was self-denial with joy, for the privilege of service. And whom will he serve? There will be no question asked as to the worthiness or unworthiness of the children that will be received into this home when established.[E]

CHAPTER XIX

RADIANCIES OF HUMOR

I want to radiate humor and my appreciation of it. But it must be natural, genuine, kind-hearted, sweet, and pure. The humor that has a sting for some one else, that is unkind, unjust, malicious, cruel, or unclean is not for me. And, furthermore, I do not want that any one should ever feel that I can or would enjoy such humor. I want to radiate such a spirit, give forth such an "aura" that no one will ever come to me with unkind or unclean humor, or expect me to want to hear it.

No, true humor is gentle, kind, humane, and human. I think little of any man or woman who cannot enjoy a good hearty laugh. I believe in laughter; in joking, in fun, in wit, in humor—in the things that provoke laughter. Laugh heartily, laugh loud, laugh long, and you will oftentimes laugh away dyspepsia, the blues, and worries. Laugh at your own misfortunes, your own mishaps. My dear friend, Burdette, used to clap me on the back and exclaim in his bright, cheery voice: "Be your own funny man." He once illustrated it by saying, in effect: "You've laughed many a time watching a man chase his hat when a windstorm ran away with it, but how do you feel when it's your own hat? Take a look at yourself. See the spectacle you make—the bewhiskered, the dignified, the long-legged—as you rush frantically after the fleeing tile. Can't you see the fun in bending down, making a dive for the hat, just at the moment an extra gust comes and—flip, flop—the hat scoots on and you grasp the empty space. Laugh at yourself, my boy, and you'll get hold of the world by the tail and conquer it!"

How true it is!

The greatest humoristic after-dinner speaker in America to-day is Simeon Ford. How often have I laughed at and with him. Study his humor. Half of it is making fun at himself, his "bizarre, gothic style of architecture," and that kind of thing. He pokes fun, slyly, at himself, and watches the effect on other people. Instead of "guying" other, and sensitive, people—(notice, I say sensitive, *not* sensible),—he guys himself, and the more absurd the picture he can draw of himself the more he seems to enjoy it. He is original, quaint, individualistic, truly funny, not a mere retailer of old chestnuts, warmed over at the brazier of his wit, but a creator, a real *maker* of humor, and the result is people sit and laugh and laugh, and then laugh some more, and when it is all over go away wondering what it was all about. But there is no sarcasm, no sting, no malice in the fun, no one is hurt, everything is as harmless as the frolics of a young lamb.

So it was with dear little Marshall Wilder. Dear Marsh! how I loved him! Handicapped with a distorted body, his mind was as quick as lightning. How well I remember running in upon him in his bedroom in a hotel in Buffalo one morning and asking him to come down to a breakfast table of friends who had assembled to give me a "Good-by." Though he was not well, he hastily threw on his clothes, came down, and for an hour brightened our circle, with some of the most flashing, bright, and spontaneous wit I ever heard. Everybody was charmed, delighted, thrilled, for he sprang from gay to grave, laughter to tears, jollity to pathos so startlingly quick as to keep us with one hand to our eyes, wiping away the tears, when we had originally raised them to hide our wide-open, laughing mouths. He loved to make others happy; he was ever ready to plunge deep into the pool of simple-hearted pure fun. Who will ever forget that day when he, Elbert Hubbard, Von Liebich, with half a dozen or more of the brightest minds of the Continent, who were visiting at Roycroft together, planned to go to the Pan-American Exposition at Buffalo. I was privileged to be of the number. We planned to go as a lot of country joskins, real "Hicks," with hayseed in our hair, and carrying our carpet-bags with us. As I was the only bewhiskered man of the "bunch," I was made the victim. I was to dress in country style, go down the "Midway"—or whatever the street of shows was called—and attract the attention of the "barkers" and draw their fire. Then the others were to saunter up and we, in turn, would open up our fire upon the barker. Can you imagine the results? We carried out the plan exactly as contemplated. I ate liquorice and let the juice flow down from the corners of my mouth, so that it looked like tobacco juice, I gaped at everything, and listened with wide-eyed wonder, I felt like a countryman, so now I looked like one, and I became, immediately, the butt of the jokes and jests of the "spieler" of the show before which I stood. I think I can fairly hold my own in such a combat, and the audience that was assembled, generally seemed to think so, but imagine the way the fur began to fly when Hubbard arrived and chipped in, and Marshall and Von, and Bert II, and each of the others. Talk about a stranger dog set on by a dozen home dogs—it was nothing, compared with the fun we had badgering and baiting that over-confident spieler. Then I moved on to the next stand, far enough away, however, so that no one was aware of our plot. The crowd soon "tumbled" and followed, and we repeated the game to the infinite amazement of the discomfited "barkers." It was the wildest revelry of good-natured, good-humored, spontaneous fun I have ever engaged in, and a thousand years can never efface its memory.

Dignity! What had we to do with dignity? We were fun-makers, delight-makers, like the old-time Indians of the cliff-dwelling days, and we went into the game with vim, energy, earnestness, abandon, and enthusiasm.

And I learned a wonderful lesson, once, from Marshall Wilder, that was worth many a long-winded sermon for practical usefulness in meeting the hardships, the woes, the pains of life. I was on the stage of a theater with him, just preparatory to his "act." He was suffering excruciating agony—as he often did, from his frail and deformed body—and sweat was pouring down his brow and cheeks. "Put your arms around me, and love me tight, George!" he gasped, "hold me tight," and I held him, clasping his hands also in mine. He gripped me with fierce intensity, clearly indicating the pain he was in, and thus we stood, until the call came for him. Then, wiping his brow and face, with a smile that was at once ghastly and sweet in its pathos, he rushed before his audience, and had them laughing at his merry quips and quirks, his jests and jokes, before I could recover from the sympathy I felt for his deep suffering. Brave, courageous, plucky Marsh. Ready to make fun for others in spite of his own pain. How often when men come to me with long drawn-out tales of their woes, *their* pains, *their* sufferings, *their* trials, *their* hardships, do I feel like saying to them: "Cut it out! Go and do as did Marsh Wilder. Make some one else laugh. Make some one else happy, and you'll forget your own troubles!" For it is true. The very effort of concentration upon making others laugh, or add to their happiness, largely, if not completely, leads to a forgetfulness of one's own woes.

Then, too, the man who can laugh at himself wins a hearing from the world that nothing else can gain for him. There is an appeal, somehow, in this fact, that is irresistible. Bishop Peck, of the M. E. Church, was a Falstaffian build of man. Indeed, it is said that he weighed a full pound for every day in the year. A man with three hundred and sixty-five pounds of corporeal presence naturally possessed an aldermanic "front" of compelling proportions. On one occasion the Bishop was called upon at the General Conference (which, I believe, that year met in Baltimore), to represent the church upon the Pacific Coast. The good bishop had a habit of always stroking, or smoothing down his vest, when beginning his address, and at this time, as he arose, and began his deliberate strokings of his vast and protuberant rotundity, he accompanied it with the words: "Brethren, the Pacific Slope greets you!"

His amazement, as a perfect roar of laughter greeted him and shook the building, can well be imagined, yet he did not lose his *sang-froid*. In another moment he had grasped the fun of the situation, and laughing with the vast audience, seized upon that as a theme upon which he played with eloquence, fervor, and power in an extemporized speech which, as many who heard it say, he never surpassed in his life.

Suppose his "dignity" had prevented his joining in the laugh at himself! What an opportunity he would have lost.

I saw a similar event once in the Free Trade Hall, in Manchester, England. That great assembly hall was crowded, awaiting the coming upon the platform of the Conference of all the Baptist Ministers of Great Britain. We had been waiting some time and I, for one, was young enough to be impatient as the time announced drew near. It was in the days of Moody and Sankey's great revivals in England, and Sankey's hymn, "Hold the Fort!" had captured the church-going ear. To pass away the time I started the song. The audience caught on. We sang the first verse and the chorus with vim and fervor. Then, just as we began the second verse, the body of ministers began to march on to the platform, led by their gray-haired president. Recall the lines and imagine the result as the words of the marching ministers were united in our thoughts!

> See the mighty host advancing
> Satan leading on!

Some of us shrieked with laughter. One man near me nearly had a fit of hysterics. They say Englishmen can't see a joke. I never saw an American audience "catch on" any quicker than did that Manchester one. In a moment the singing stopped and the place was in an uproar of wildest laughter. The good president at first seemed nonplused and confused, but some one must have explained it to him, for before the ministers had scarce taken their seats, he advanced to the edge of the platform, secured silence, and began to the effect: "Beloved friends! If we seem like the hosts of evil, marching with Satan at their head, we belie our looks. The Evil One has blinded your eyes. We are the army of the other side. We are Christian soldiers, engaged in a never-to-cease conflict with that army of evil that we shall assuredly conquer," and so on, giving one of the most pertinent, direct, spontaneous, and truly eloquent of addresses.

He rose to the occasion—joined in the laugh upon himself, won his audience, and then used the sympathy he had gained, to strike home some deep and important truths.

This is what I want to live, to radiate: love of humor, readiness to laugh at it even though it be laughing at myself, ready to make it when I can for others, ready to join in other people's appreciation of it.

CHAPTER XX

RADIANCIES OF THE "ETERNAL NOW"

Is there any past, any future, in our lives? If I look back upon the past, or anticipate the future, whether with joy or pleasure, do I not do it in the *now*? To-morrow never comes, for when it arrives it is no longer to-morrow,—it is *now*. Life is one *eternal now*. The great trouble, however, with most people, is that they have not learned that fact. They do not live in the *now*, they sit down and lament over the past; weep that its joys are gone, its glories faded, altogether oblivious of the resplendent beauties that now surround them, the radiant joyousnesses that environ them, NOW. Or, they sit in fond anticipation, in expectation, with impatient waiting for to-morrow, for next week, for next year, ignoring the immediate and present sweet singing of the birds, the exquisite daintiness of the flowers, their delicate fragrance, the majesty and sublimity of the snowy mountain peaks, the upright stateliness of the trees, the supernal clarity of the sky, the pellucidness of the atmosphere, the champagne-like quality of the air, NOW.

What time we lose, waste, pervert, by forgetting the duty, the joy, the delight of living in the Eternal Now. Take your joys as they come along. It is the Divine plan that every moment shall be filled with His joy—the joy of living, of being.

Eyes are given to see with *now*! Are you using them now? Do you gaze upon the grass, the trees, the flitting butterflies, the busy insects, the bees, the beautiful birds, the clouds, the sky, the sea, the rippling cascades, the *everything* of Nature, NOW, and enjoy their many-formed, many-hued, many-graced splendors.

Ears are given for hearing *now*!

Are yours alert for all the sweet, the pleasant, the comforting, the joyous, the sublime sounds that might come to them now? Or are you like the "fools and blind" who will sit at a Boston Symphony concert and gabble gossip or retail slander?

Palates are given to taste with *now*!

Are you tasting the apples, the rare lusciousness of grapes, peaches, oranges, plums, and the thousand and one delicate fruits *now*, or are you regretting the lost truffles, the sauces, the spices, the wines, the stimulating things of yesterday, or longing for the Lucullus repasts of to-morrow?

Oh, the content and happiness of taking joys as they come, in their simpleness and naturalness, in their every-day, common, normal order; of looking for them, expecting them, anticipating them, going out, as it were, to meet them.

Is it only a walk of ten blocks (or five) to the store, or office, or school? Are you ready as you step out of your door to inhale the fragrance of the morning air, or enjoy its own peculiar delight if the morning is wet, misty, foggy, rainy? Do you see the moving and sun-lit clouds; the clear sky, the rustling leaves of the trees; the hopping of the happy birds; the joyousness of the children walking to school?

Be alert, receptive, ready. Seize the *small joy of the now*, and you will find it far more delightful than all the anticipations, and even the realizations of what seem to be the *large joys of the to-morrow*.

One of the saddest pictures on canvas to me is one called "The Pursuit of Pleasure." It represents a female figure as *Pleasure*, floating through the air, and followed by an eager crowd of men and women, of all ages and conditions in life. Reaching, grasping, breathless, regardless of their tramplings upon each other, indifferent that some of their whilom companions are fallen and cannot arise, and that hopeless despair is depicted in their eyes and faces, each and all of the remaining strugglers fix their eyes upon the phantom though alluring figure. And thus the pursuit goes on continuously; there is no reaching her; she is ever illusive and evasive, a delusion and a snare, ever beckoning yet ever retreating.

In her sculptured fountain at the Panama-Pacific Exposition, Mrs. Harry Payne Whitney expresses the same idea, but even more forcefully than does the picture. Here are thirty-seven figures nearly all intent upon reaching their goal of happiness. They cannot even see what it is. Yet the eagerness depicted upon the faces, in the straining attitudes, the strenuous striving in that one direction, all typify the desire, the intentness, the resolute pursuit of happiness. Then, alas, when the doors are reached, they are both found closed, guarded by Assyrian and Egyptian figures, that suggest the occult mystery of the beyond, and that look down sternly and unyieldingly upon the two figures at their feet, long strivers, evidently pleading for the admission that is denied them. There are two definite, distinct, and different ways in which these two allegories can be interpreted. One is that mankind ever lives in the world of the senses, pursuing the gratifications of the now, the feastings, the drinkings, the carousings, the pleasuring, the wantonings of the sense-life, the sensual life, and that such a pursuit is ever doomed to failure, for man—the spiritual, created in God's own image—can never be satisfied with the temporary things of earth and sense.

The other interpretation is that man is ever seeking for some *far-off*, great, *extraordinary* pleasure, joy, or satisfaction, something in the future, rather than living in the smaller joys of the *now*. The child longs to be the youth or maiden, enjoying "sitting up at nights," "going to parties," "eating candies," "going out with the boys," "smoking like a man"; the youth eagerly works for the time when he shall be his own master, control his own business; the maiden, have her lover, marry successfully, become the mistress of her own house; the grown man looks forward to and works desperately for the time when he shall have "made his pile," and the woman to "an assured place in society." These, and a thousand and one "*pursuits*" engage men and women.

In my own life I am eagerly desirous to radiate the opposite of both of these conceptions. I certainly do not wish to belong to the class pictured in Christ's parable of the rich man; he who thought only of the so-called good things of this life which he would enjoy now—he who said: "Let us eat, drink, and be merry, for to-morrow we die." The slightest observation of life, of the men and women one meets daily, soon convinces one of the hollowness, the dissatisfaction, the incompleteness of all earthly things. The subject is too trite to need any amplification. Yet, the wonder of it is, that, in spite of this fact, the great majority of people still thus strive for wealth, place, power, honor, social success, possessions, attainments. Why is it that this *ignis fatuus* has such power of allurement? Why is it that men and women are so foolish, so slow to rule their actions by their own inner spiritual awakenings, rather than the habits and fashions followed by others?

I have no desire or ambition for fame, for honor, for success, for place, for power, *as such*. They are useless to me save as I may use them for the benefit, the happiness, the pleasure of my fellows. I am slowly awakening to the realization of what I believe now to be a primal fact, viz., that all a man can really hold and enjoy in his living hand, in his soul, in his life, is that which he gives away, shares, distributes among his fellows.

Elsewhere I have quoted Joaquin Miller's lines from *Peter Cooper*:

> For all you can hold in your dead, cold hand,
> Is what you have given away.

I now wish to radiate my belief in the enlargement of that idea as stated above. Even knowledge can give no real satisfaction unless shared, given to others; the joy of a picture owned is lost unless others can enjoy with you. In other words, the possession of anything *for self alone* is destructive of happiness. One learns slowly but surely that even in these things of the mind and the soul:

> That man who lives for self alone
> Lives for the meanest mortal known.

CHAPTER XXI

RADIANCIES OF EXTREMES

Life is made up of extremes and everything that comes between them. There is the North Pole and there is the South Pole. There is the heat of the fiery furnace and the cold of the Arctic Zone. There is the height of heaven and the depth of hell; the voice of the thunder and the whisper of the gentle zephyr.

Man is a singular being. He is as diverse as is the manifold face of Nature upon which he gazes. His likes and dislikes are many and varied. Men of equal intelligence and equal powers differ in their ways of looking at the same thing. The poet Browning effectively states this when he says:

> Ten men love what I hate,
> Shun what I follow, slight what I receive;
> Ten, who in ears and eyes
> Match mine.

In the face of such facts one is compelled to the conclusion that personal idiosyncrasy or individual preference alone can decide what it wants, needs, and must have, in this large diversity that is offered it.

The fact that ten men who have equal powers of observation and reflection as myself love the things that I hate, and reject the things that I receive, has absolutely no influence in deciding me in regard to the things that I hate and receive, any more than the fact that I hate and receive things to which they have the antagonistic feeling influences them; hence it is useless for me to attempt to enforce my likings and antipathies upon others, even as it is useless for them to attempt to force theirs upon me.

So I have been led to accept the philosophy, which I wish to radiate to all men, that it appears to me the Divine Wisdom has provided for these personal idiosyncrasies of human nature by giving to us the extremes of things with everything that lies between. So, regardless of my own preference, I believe that the strong wind is as much a beneficent force of Nature as is the zephyr; the thundering cataract of Yosemite as the placid Mirror Lake; the avalanche as the snowflake; the thunder as the violet; the earthquake as the rippling rill; the blazing meteor as the Milky Way; the flaming sun-spots as the sparkling dewdrop; the fiery volcano as the quiet glowworm; the giant sequoia as the tiny forget-me-not; the thundering breakers of ocean as the gentle pattering raindrop; the fiery boiling geyser as the silently flowing fountain; the dazzling comet as the serene fixed star; the rugged Grand Canyon as the flower-besprinkled sward; the monster whale as the tiny gold-fish; the giant elephant as the timid mouse; the blaring trumpet as the soothing guitar; the startling kettle-drum as the smoothly flowing 'cello; the clanging cymbals as the seductive oboe.

I firmly believe and wish to radiate my belief that God has as much use for the man of the farm as for the man of the drawing-room; the rudeness of "The man with the hoe" as the smoothness of the man with the higher education. He needs the arid desert as well as the fertile plain; the wild ruggedness of the ravine as well as the cultivated garden; the colorless abysses of the glacier as well as the flower-besprinkled foothills. He has use for the snowy plains of the north as well as the rice fields of the south; the cactus as well as the orchid; the giant suaharo as well as the shrinking gilia; the prickly pear, as the velvety peach; the sword-fish, as the nautilus; the shark as the flying-fish; the flaming sunrises and sunsets, as the tender tints of the lily, and the night-blooming cereus; the deep purples, as well as the blush rose; the glowing yellows as the softer blues; the piercing greens as the quieter violets. The bluffs and promontories that thrust their heads out into the ocean are as much a part of God's great out-of-doors and of as much use as are the placid landscapes; the mountain heights as much needed as are the flower-bespangled levels; the vast reaches of prairie as the secluded and confined valley. The piercing cold of the Arctic has as much a place in Nature as the alluring mildness of Southern California or the Riviera; the monster tides of the Bay of Fundy as the ripples of the placid pool.

The sturdy and warlike Viking has as much a place in history as the diplomatic and artistic Italian; the Negro as the Caucasian; the Chinaman as the French; the Oriental as the English; the Japanese as the American.

El Capitan and Gibraltar are not exquisitely carved statues by Canova or Thorwaldsen, but they have just as much a place in the history of the world's development.

The wilds of the high Sierras, in all their rude and majestic splendor, rugged and tremendous vastness, where clear-eyed, horny-handed, strong-oathed, and rudely clad men wander and labor, are very different from the city drawing-rooms,—those places of pink teas and white kid-gloved men and women; those breeding places of superficial conventionality and effete conceptions of people and life, but I doubt not that the high Sierras have produced more of benefit to mankind than all the drawing-rooms of all the civilizations.

I love the pastoral and quiet landscapes of the Connecticut River Valley, of placid Killarney, of the quiet vale of Avoca, of picturesque Normandy, but the passion, power, majesty, sublimity, solitude, dreariness and desolation of the far-reaching Colorado Desert, deep descending Grand Canyon, bold escarpments of the Red Rock country, and other tremendous and solitary places of Nature command me, allure me, appeal to me, and dominate me quicker than the quiet places of beauty.

What, in Nature, to some men is the end of things to others is the beginning. The sacred writer says that God even "maketh the wrath of men to praise him," as well as their love and tenderness.

Life is not all comprised about a slender figure and transparent profile; faultless coils of hair; soft, rich, clinging garments; laces falling over taper fingers; graceful and dignified demeanor; low and sweetly modulated voice, and the perfection of faultless manners. There may be a place for the rude, uncouth clodhopper with disfigured features; tousled hair; clad in homespun or cheap denim; rags taking the place of lace; boorish and clumsy demeanor; a voice like a steamer foghorn; and the apotheosis of all that is blundering and awkward in manner.

I do not, for one moment, defend any unnecessary boorishness or uncouthness of manner, and must not be understood as doing so, but at the same time, in spite of these things, I am impelled to state my conviction that the latter class is more needful to the real progress of the world than the former. I notice that several times in the history of the world, canal-drivers, shepherd-boys, wood-choppers, and rail-splitters have made wonderful pilots for the Ship of State.

God has use in His world for the rough as well as the polished; the roar of the thunder as well as the coo of the dove; the stentorian trumpet-tone as well as the still, small voice. John the Baptist came from the desert robed in skins and camel's hair; his voice, doubtless, was not soft and well-modulated as were those of Herodias and Salome. He was "the voice of one crying in the wilderness." His call contained the thunder tones of the storm and wild cry of the lonely eagle seeking its solitary aerie; the strength and the roar of the lion. It was neither refined, pleasing, nor cultured, but it possessed life and power and it was chosen to herald the coming of the Messiah.

Nowhere have we been told that Elijah, Jeremiah and Daniel were noted for the soft and dulcet tones of their voices, yet they were the chosen instruments of the Divine in overthrowing dynasties and changing the history of nations. Peter the Hermit was not a sweet-voiced singer in Israel, but he started a movement that led to the civilization of Europe. I doubt not that the charges of the British against Joan of Arc that she cried in a coarse military voice when she led the armored hosts of France were true, but she drove the foreign invader from the soil of her beloved France where they had held footing for nigh upon a hundred years and no one else had been able to win a victory from them.

I doubt not there were times when Grant's voice did not possess the mellow and refined quality of the drawing-room exquisite, but he won victories and made a united people possible. John Brown was rude, rough, uncouth, boorish, when compared with the refined and polished cavaliers of the South. They called him a bandit, an invader, a revolutionist, an anarchist, and they captured and hanged him, but to thousands of men his crazy dream of the invasion of the South to forcibly compel the freedom of the slave is being more and more seen by hundreds of thousands of wise men to have been one of the most practical and effective means of calling the attention of men to the moral principle involved in the question of slavery, as to whether men of one color of blood or skin had the right to hold in bondage men of a different color.

When Theodore Parker was denouncing the iniquities of any and all slavery, his voice was not as soft and gentle and sweetly modulated as that of Longfellow, yet it played as important a part in the history of the development of mankind and stirred men to higher endeavor on the part of their suffering and down-trodden fellows.

What, then, is the upshot of the whole matter? It seems to me it is this: Listen to the voice that appeals to your own soul; that lifts you from the lower to the higher; that thrills you to deeds of heroism, that stimulates you to acts of nobleness, that calls you to a life of helpful self-sacrifice; and while doing this, cease to criticise, to find fault, to censure the kind of voice to which you do not care to listen. The strong, vigorous, robust, red-blooded man of the out-of-doors generally will not speak nor act with the perfect restraint and conventionality of the man born in the atmosphere of the drawing-room, but his message may be just as helpful to the world, and as divinely inspired as that of his more refined and dignified prototype.

CHAPTER XXII

ABSORPTION IN RELATION TO RADIATION

Most important factors in Living the Radiant Life are Living the Life of *Possession* and Living the Absorptive Life. To radiate one must possess, and to possess one must absorb. To give largely and well, one must receive largely and well. The Absorptive Life is as essential as the Radiant Life. Out in the great silences are the eloquent voices of God ready to speak to the attentive soul; out in Nature a million voices are ready to impart knowledge to the ignorant. All one has to do to receive is to "ask"; not with the voice but with the whole being. As a sponge absorbs water up to the limit of its capacity, so should man absorb, and then, unlike the sponge, which must be squeezed from without ere it will give off that which it has received, man should radiate from within all that he has received.

There are few people in the world who are true absorbers. We are so full of prejudices, conceits, notions, that we refuse to receive from this, that, or the other source, because, forsooth, we in our pride deem the source unworthy. The true life receives from every source. Call nothing unclean. All things are yours. God is over and in all. Prove all things. Open your heart to all good from whatever source. Stand humbly before God ready to receive. Keep your hands open; your eyes, your ears, your nostrils, your whole nature in a state of active receptivity. Be afraid of nothing. Some one comes and tells you that in this or that he has found spiritual life and help. You, however, have been taught to regard that as a dangerous thing, so you are afraid of it. Arise and be above such fears. Are you a man, a woman, a human soul, made in the image of God and given powers of thought, of discernment, of decision? Or are you a mere puppet to be worked by the string of other men's thoughts, other men's ideas, other men's opinions? Listen for yourself; think for yourself; decide for yourself; act for yourself. If a thing seems right to your own soul do it though the heavens fall and you suffer the condemnation of all mankind. True and rapid progress will never come to the race until individual men learn that they alone are the arbiters of their own destiny.

Go out into Nature, into the silences, into the workshops and the marts of trade *and absorb.* Listen to every good voice that speaks, and if you are not sure whether the voice is good or not, listen anyhow and "prove" it by the infallible tests of purity, unselfishness, and uplift.

Every human soul may be a wireless telegraph receiver. God is flashing out messages every moment from His million and one instruments all over the universe. They are all kinds of messages—but all from the one spirit, and therefore all spiritual. They appeal to the bodies, the minds, the souls of men, and all you have to do to receive them is to have your receiving apparatus of body, mind, and soul attuned to the sending apparatus of the Loving Sender. Get in tune. Cry out to God: I want all there is. I cast aside all prejudgments, all conceits, all ideas. Let me hear direct from Thee. Go out into the fields and receive from the spirit that is in, over, and about Nature. Every tree, flower, grass, bird, insect, animal, cloud, storm, rock, stream has a message for you if you will but hear it. Love alone can open your heart to receive; it is the key with which the soul and mind and body are set in tune. Get yourself into *relationship* with Nature. Feel your kinship. God is the Father of every tree as much as he is your Father. Go and claim your family. And claim all the good they possess as your own, for it is yours and merely awaits your taking. As a child you did this with your mother. The nourishment of her breasts, the gentle hush of her voice, the soothing touch of her fingers, the brooding yearning of her love; all these were yours the moment you cried out for them. Mother Nature is as full of the spirit of Love as your physical mother. Indeed the latter is one in spirit with the former. Call out then. Demand, with the simple expectancy of the child, all that you need. Call for it confident that it will come. Expect it, and according to your expectancy it will be given unto you.

But to do this you must be a true child of your Nature Mother. You must confidently lean on her breast, you must confidently blend yourself with her, you must let her touch you as your mother used to touch you when, a helpless babe, you lay in your cradle. Her hand went all over your body, from head to foot, with loving, soothing caress. Let the sun and the breezes touch your body in like fashion. Their fingers will soothe with mesmeric power and at the same time bring health and strength and vigor, and withal, peace. Go and lie down on the bosom of the Earth Mother; feel her pulsating heart, and in time, when you have forgotten your artificiality and pretension, your so-called civilization and culture, and found anew your kinship with the Earth, you will feel the whole power of Nature pulsing through your veins; the fever of your unhealthy blood will be soothed and it will flow naturally and coolly as the sweet sap that ascends to the nourishment of the topmost branch and leaf.

And when life has wounded you, cut you, torn you almost limb from limb, and you feel and see yourself only an almost dismembered trunk, Nature will soothe and heal you. Your wounds will soon be scarred over and the trees, the ferns, the birds, the grasses, the squirrels, the bees, the buds, the blossoms, and the butterflies,—all—will associate with you on equal terms. They will neither laugh at you nor repel you, but as loving friends come and associate with you in sweet and dear kinship. You will walk through the aisled forest temples of God repentant and forgiven for sins of the past, and shame and sorrow will flee away, replaced by the calm joy of the peace that flows into the receiving heart like a river. You will undress and bathe in the sunshine and the pools, the creeks and the rivers, fearless and unabashed, for you will have exposed your soul to the soul of things; real shame has nothing to do with externals.

But, you ask, how am I to begin to observe and thus absorb the good gifts of God into my very life in order that I may live and radiate them to others? Let me help you to begin!

To be satisfied is to stagnate and petrify. In his *Rabbi Ben Ezra*, Robert Browning has three pregnant lines:

> What I aspired to be,
> And was not, comforts me:
> A brute I might have been, but would not sink i' the scale.

The aspiring soul is the one reaching out to absorb. One might be a satisfied brute by closing all the avenues of aspiration and high ambition, but it is immeasurably better to be an unsatisfied, aspiring man rather than the satisfied low-minded brute.

Aspiration is the hunger of the soul. Hunger implies need. So foster—cultivate—your hunger. The hungry seek for food, and food gives new life, new growth, new strength, new power. The Universe of God is full of food for man's mind and soul. And it is of infinite variety, capable of nourishing myriads of soul-powers that now lie dormant in your nature. Awaken to your needs. Be on the lookout every moment for the free gifts of God that hang from the trees of life that grow in every back yard as well as on high mountains and in every fertile orchard.

There is a great deal more in this expression, "cultivate a hunger," than at first sight appears. People who satisfy their lower appetites know nothing of the true hunger of the soul. And consequently when they see the food designed by the Almighty Love and Wisdom to satisfy to the full all the demands of true hunger, these grossly contented minds pass them by, their eyes are closed so that they see not; their senses are dulled so that they smell not, hear not, feel not, taste not. I have seen people fast from every kind of food, solid or liquid, for ten, twenty, thirty or forty, and in one case even for eighty days. At the end of these fasts, the fasters related with delight their keen pleasure and satisfaction at realizing what real hunger was as differentiated from the mere appetite for food that they had felt prior to their fasts. As a rule we eat too much. We satiate ourselves upon foods that are not always good for us, and thus destroy the true normal appetite for pure, good, healthful, simple foods.

Among these people who fasted were several who were thin and poorly nourished, and yet who had abnormal appetites and ate far more food than those who were robust, hearty, vigorous, and strong. The physician said, what was self-evident, that the more food they ate, the less nourished they became, because they overloaded themselves with food and much of it was the wrong kind. It was hard work for these people to fast, but at the close of the fast, their abnormal and unnatural appetite had disappeared and in its stead had come a true, normal hunger which revealed to them the right kind of food that they should eat to satisfy the demands of the body and which, when they did eat, was immediately assimilated. The result was that within a month or two, after having learned what real hunger was as differentiated from perverted appetite, they were fat and rosy, plump and vigorous, beautiful and energetic.

It is exactly the same in our mental and spiritual life. We feed upon the grosser foods to satiation and repletion and the result is that we suffer from mental and spiritual dyspepsia and are pale, thin, anæmic and weak, where we should be beautiful, vigorous, energetic, and strong. Quit stuffing and craving the lower foods. Stay away from the theater, the vaudeville, the cheap show. Quit reading the sensational novel, the trashy story of excitement. Give your brain, your mind, your soul, a rest. Fast a while. Do as Elijah did, as Jesus, as Mahomet. Go into the desert, the solitude, and for forty days and nights rest, body, mind, and soul, until real hunger takes possession of you. Then come forth and begin to absorb from all the great wealth of God that surrounds you.

There are three chief sources of purest mind and soul supply and I wish briefly to consider each one of these. They are: 1. Observation. 2. Reading. 3. Intuition.

This may not be a scientific classification, but it suffices for my purpose. I have not put the most important first, but observation is the one man most relies upon.

1. Observation is God's method of filling up the inner supply of man's knowledge through the senses. He sees, feels, hears, smells, tastes, and through these avenues receives mental impressions. One can observe the lower things or the higher. Every day as I ride on the train or street cars, I observe men reading their newspapers. As a rule I can tell in a few minutes what a man's mental hunger is by watching him read. He chooses the pink sheet and devours with avidity the stories of prize fights. He turns to the pages devoted to courts and reads the accounts of murder trials or of scenes where lawyers quarrel or jangle and where witnesses testify to disgusting and loathsome things. Another man is interested in clean athletics and reads with interest of college football, Marathon games, and the like. Still another is absorbed in the news of a higher nature, a meeting of the Hague Peace Conference, the endeavors of statesmen to bring about a better understanding between the North and the South, between nations. In other words, a man takes what his appetite craves out of the newspaper. Just so it is with all life. Men take whatever their appetites crave. If the appetite is false, unnatural, abnormal, they take injurious food. Only when the depraved appetite becomes changed into natural, normal hunger, is the right kind of food sought and found. Yet there is immeasurably more of the pure, good food to satisfy the perfect, normal hunger, than there is of the carrion which the vulture instincts in us crave.

2. Reading. While I have put this under a separate head, it really belongs under the head of observation, for the reading of books is but observation of

the observations of other men. Yet, as I shall show later, this is a special field which one should endeavor to glean with care.

3. Intuition. To the really normally hungry soul, this is the chief, indeed, the only source of spiritual food. It is what Emerson called the "Oversoul," and what Doctor Buck meant when, in speaking of Walt Whitman, he said he possessed the "cosmic conscience." It is receptiveness to universal truth, Divine truth, that truth which knows no time, no place, no boundaries of nationality, no difference in creed, in sect, in sex, in color, but that, like the sun, shines alike upon all, whether bond or free, rich or poor, learned or unlearned, black, white, brown, or red, savage or civilized. It is the spirit that possessed—in varying degrees—Gautama, Buddha, Confucius, Mahomet, Jesus, Joan of Arc, Emerson, Browning, Whitman, all great souls who have seen the truth universal and recorded it for the uplift and ennobling of mankind.

May I here suggest a few ideas as to how you should begin to absorb the good things of God in order to get the fullest benefit from them, and then let us go out together and absorb some of the things that will make one a newer, fuller, more vigorous and truly radiant being.

Get into the habit of looking out of your bedroom window at the skies each night before you retire to rest. Is it clear? Study that brilliant scheme of stars and planets. What grander sight could you ask for? Yet every common man and woman may see it from the smallest attic or hall-bedroom window. Is the moon in the heavens dimming the stars but flooding the earth with dream-light? Can you see the great wonderful clouds floating about in the night's silences away up under the light of the moon or against the sparkling of the far off stars? Or is the sky dark and lowering with black clouds so that you can see nothing as yet? What a wonderful thing that cloud screen is; that soft, moist vapor piled in great billows above us, shutting out the heavens and their wonders from our gaze. How dark it seems on the earth beneath. How shut away from the brightness and serenity of the stars. Yet we know that the clouds are but temporary, that they will soon pass over, and that we are perfectly safe nestling here on the quiet bosom of mother earth.

Look up to the heavens *every night* for some intellectual and spiritual food, just as you go to the dining-room, *only more so*. Form the habit!

Study the stars as David did. They are as free to you as they were to him. The poorest beggar and the most degraded sot have as much claim to the stars as the king on his throne or the most divine man that ever lived. What a wonderful drama is being nightly played in the skies. How much more interesting and attractive to the seeing and understanding eye than the puppet shows of the theater, where there is so much of the glare, the tinsel, the sham, the shoddy.

The Passion Play of Oberammergau is well worth seeing. To witness and hear the dramas of Wagner is worth while, especially soul-stirring *Parsifal*, but here in the heavens is the great mystery of the Creator, watched over, guarded, protected by these bright armored knights,—the stars and the planets, the comets, the nebulæ, the milky way,—with a vigilance which is as keen as it is eternal.

A thoughtful girl once wrote me to the effect that after she first began to realize the glories of the stars, she prayed to a different God from the God she had always associated with formality, churches, prayer books, creeds, and the communion service. She said, in effect, that her prayer became less glib, less wordy, less ready, for the stars inspired her with the sense of majesty and awe of the Great Creator, so that she came before Him with words that meant more even though they came with less smoothness of utterance. Awe will take the place of smug self-satisfaction; the obeisance of the soul to mere bending of the knees; an all-sweeping passion for uplift rather than vain repetitions and selfish cries for more of the baubles of life to play with. There is no doubt whatever that Tennyson had some such thoughts in mind when he wrote in *Locksley Hall*:

> Many a night from yonder ivied casement, ere I went to rest,
> Did I look on great Orion sloping slowly to the West.
> Many a night I saw the Pleiads, rising through the mellow shade,
> Glitter like a swarm of fireflies tangled in a silver braid.

Longfellow, too, has an exquisite poem on *The Light of the Stars*:

> The night has come, but not too soon;
>   And sinking silently,
> All silently, the little moon
>   Drops down behind the sky.

There is no light in earth or heaven
   But the cold light of stars;
And the first watch of night is given
   the red planet Mars.

Is it the tender star of love?
   The star of love and dreams?
O no! from that blue tent above,
   A hero's armor gleams.

And earnest thoughts within me rise,
   When I behold afar,
Suspended in the evening skies,
   The shield of that red star.

O star of strength! I see thee stand
   And smile upon my brain;
Thou beckonest with thy mailed hand,
   And I am strong again.

Within my heart there is no light
   But the cold light of stars;
I give the first watch of the night
   To the red planet Mars.

The star of the unconquered will
   He rises in my heart
Serene, and resolute, and still,
   And calm, and self-possessed.

And thou, too, whosoe'er thou art,
   That readest this brief psalm,
As one by one thy hopes depart,
   Be resolute and calm.

O fear not in a world like this,
   And thou shalt know ere long,
Know how sublime a thing it is

> To suffer and be strong.

So study the stars, get from them all you can. Let their serenity sink into your soul, and their calm peace speak peace to your troubled and restless spirit. Yield to your imagination as to whatever they bring you, and be thankful for every suggestion of largeness, bigness, power, and love.

In his *Saul*, Browning has David tell how the stars suggested to him the life of the people far away, who dwelt far beyond the possibility of his ever seeking them. How could he, the poor and humble shepherd lad, ever hope to see and know these people? Yet he could picture them. So can you. Let your imagination grow! Let it roam! Enjoy all it gives to you of good and inspiration. Think of the life you might live if you had the power some of these people have, and then seek to live worthy of that larger life even in the restricted sphere in which you are placed.

But there are other things in the heavens, almost as common as the stars, that may become a great and glorious inspiration to you.

I once saw a display of lightning that came to me as a revelation from God. It was so vivid and intense that the friends who were with me, old Arizona pioneers who had braved hundreds of storms, were afraid, and like myself hid their faces in their blankets. But by and by the absurdity of this act struck me;—as if we were safer with our heads covered than if we were taking in the sight in all its sublimity and terrible splendor. So I resolutely cast my blanket aside, and although I had not yet gotten over the shaking of my knees, I stepped to the cabin door and enjoyed the splendid scene to the full.

Who could hope to describe this display so that others can see it, or to be believed if he even attempts to picture the intense and vivid brilliancy of that evening's marvelous fire-works? For a few moments we were enveloped in a "darkness that could be felt," and then, in a moment, what seemed to be hundreds of millions of darting, zig-zag forks of lightning struck downwards through the heavens in every direction. We were encircled in these myriad flashes of vivid violet light that almost blinded us with their brilliancy. For an hour or more this display continued. But it was a sight that I can never forget, and it gave me a new insight, and new thoughts about the glory of God.

I have sat in the grass on a summer night or have walked many a mile both in the South and in the West watching the scintillating, yet soft and delicate, light of the fireflies as they sparkled and twinkled at my feet and in the air all about me. With a sort of irregular yet rhythmic movement they opened and closed their tiny lanterns, and interested, fascinated, and thrilled me by the perfection of their simple beauty.

With equal fascination I have watched the phosphorescent glow on the ocean beach, as the great foam-crested breakers curved over and dashed shoreward, gleaming with that peculiarly weird brilliancy, altogether different from any other light known to man. It is even more fascinating when seen in the amethystine waters of the Gulf of Mexico, as the steamer plows its way through the yielding waters and casts the gleaming and phosphorescent spray from side to side in the otherwise dark and silent night.

Talk about the beauties of Nature! Once begin on such a theme and there seems to be no end. A thousand and one things crowd upon the mind begging, clamoring for utterance in this record, but space forbids. Do not say you cannot see, do not say there is nothing in your immediate surroundings for you. You cannot take a step without glimpsing beauty of some kind if your eyes are awake to observe and your heart to absorb. Only this morning the maid in "doing up my room" in the city of Chicago pointed out the beauty of the black trunks and branches of the trees in the avenue contrasted against the pure white of the snow which had just fallen. Then she remarked that even the smoky buildings were changed into something beautiful and harmonious when the snow came, and she commented upon the fact that she found beauty here that charmed, thrilled, and stimulated her soul, just as much as she did amid the much-described and certainly more glowing and picturesque scenery of California.

Here is the true spirit! Do not repine for the things that are away off and that you cannot have. Take from what you can get, or go resolutely to work to get the more desirable surroundings. But *wherever you are* absorb that which is *now* and *here* presented to you, and thus you will learn to know and appreciate greater and grander things when opportunity places them before you.

2. *Absorption through Reading.*

It must not be understood that because I am constantly urging my readers to rely upon their own observations of Nature that I do not fully appreciate the benefit books may be to them. Books form a large place in my own life, and I would regret to be separated from them. They bring into my life the inner life of all the observers, thinkers, orators, seers, poets, and prophets of the ages, and yet what are books but the records of men's observations and their thoughts upon those observations? All books are not good. There are books and books. And just as some associates are injurious, so are many books. Do not waste your time on the cheap, the trashy, the useless, and injurious. Select only those books from which you are sure you can absorb those things that will be helpful and beneficial.

Some people say they read simply for entertainment. There are times when it is well to read with this object in view. If one is weary in mind or body, the brain has been overtaxed, trouble distresses one, then it is well to seek entertainment. For entertainment and the forgetting of one's cares, troubles, and weariness will mean rest and recuperation. It is well to be able to absorb such from a book that takes away thoughts from one's self. But even at such times, choose the best books from which you may absorb those things that will enable you the better to take up the battle of life with renewed energy and courage.

Do you try to keep up with all the latest books? Why? Do you read simply to say that you have read, to be able to give expression to the usual fashionable gabble on so-called "current literature"? It is not the amount you read, but the amount of good, ennobling, and uplifting influences that you gain from your reading that makes reading worth while. No person that lives can read book after book in rapid succession and absorb therefrom anything worth while. As well sit down and eat from six o'clock in the morning until twelve o'clock at night and expect the body to be healthful as to read continually and expect the mind to be healthful. It is not eating but assimilation that builds up the body. Just so, it is not reading but mental absorption that informs the mind and strengthens the soul. One book a year, thoroughly mastered, out of which you have absorbed helpful, stimulating, invigorating, health-giving, power-producing thought and action is worth more than a thousand books swallowed whole without thought or digestion.

Joaquin Miller says that "Books are for people who do not think." Very often this is a correct statement. While it is a good thing to desire the knowledge we can gain from books, it becomes an evil thing when we gain all of our knowledge of the world around us in this fashion. If the only thoughts we have are the thoughts we get from books, books are an injury instead of a blessing; a crutch instead of an invigoration.

In his early life, Edwin Markham, the poet, had but three books, the Bible, Shakspere, and Bunyan. Yet from these three books and the contemporaneous study of the mountains, valleys, canyons, plains, orchards, gardens, ocean, sea-beach, and valleys by which he was surrounded, he absorbed thoughts and saw things that enabled him to write poems that have thrilled and benefited the world.

Sir John Lubbock a few years ago chose from all the millions of books that have been published one hundred which he claims comprises all the best literature of all the ages, and more recently still, President Eliot of Harvard compressed upon a five-foot shelf all the books that he deems necessary for the really thoughtful man to possess.

I am not prepared to accept these or any other limitations as to the books I shall possess and read, and yet I do want to urge the principle involved in them upon my readers. Learn to do your own thinking rather than take your thoughts at second hand from what some one else has written. At the same time I would urge upon you the reading of the writings of our great poets that you may absorb from them their love of Nature. In this way it may be that you will be won to the love and appreciation of that which you have never before known or enjoyed. Just as the artist on his canvas sets forth for us a beautiful scene out of the great world that surrounds us and thus focalizes our attention upon it, and teaches us to see the beauty which hitherto we had passed unobserved, so does the poet focalize our attention upon that which hitherto we had passed by and neglected.

Let us read, therefore, by all means, but not as an end in itself. Let us read that thereby we may be stimulated to go out into Nature to see, feel, and absorb for ourselves. Many of the books that are "worth while" were written by men and women who have been close observers of Nature.

It is by observation that we absorb the facts and lessons of Nature. Some of the most helpful and beautiful books have been written as the result of the exercise of this faculty combined with the reflection that always comes to the truly thoughtful. The sciences are based upon observation, and as soon as one becomes interested in any particular line of study it is amazing how many fascinating things begin to crowd upon his attention. The great scientist, Agassiz, said that he could find enough to thoroughly and completely fill the whole of a life of eighty years in as much as he could cover with his one hand. I have spent night after night with astronomers whose whole vocation was to study the heavens and learn the wonderful lessons revealed thereby. One of the happiest epochs of my life was to spend two months in the High Sierras of California with Joseph Le Conte, the great geologist, and his keen and trained eyes revealed to me things in Nature that I had never seen before, and life has ever since been richer and fuller because of the experience.

Darwin studied the facts of development of plant and animal life until he wrote a book which has completely revolutionized the thought of the world. He spent years in studying the movements and influences upon the ground of the common earth-worm and showed us how great a friend to humanity is this apparently insignificant and useless creature.

Sir John Lubbock, the eminent statesman and philosopher, busy with the affairs of city and nation, spent years in studying the actions and life of the tiny ant and has given us most fascinating accounts of what he saw with philosophical deductions therefrom.

The Audubons spent their lives in studying the animals and birds of North America and their books have been a source of intense delight and instruction to all those that have been privileged to read them and see their marvelous illustrations.

Michelet, the great French scholar, studied the bee and then wrote a book about this busy insect that is as fascinating as a romance and as thrilling and interesting as a drama.

John Ward Stimson studied the various forms of snow crystals, salts, of rock substances; the natural forms of leaves, their systems of veins; the spines of the various cactuses; the marking on the furs of animals and the backs of reptiles, snakes, lizards, toads, etc.; indeed, all the multi-form shapes, spirals, curves, angles, lines, etc., of Nature, and wrote a book on them entitled *The Gate Beautiful* which one great critic and poet affirms is the greatest book, outside of the Bible and Shakspere, the world has ever known. And thus might I go on page after page, merely suggesting what men with the seeing eye and understanding heart have given to the world as the result of their observations of Nature.

Who would not observe in this fashion? Who would not like thus to fill up the mind and the soul with such wonderful facts and beautiful truths deduced therefrom?

Henry D. Thoreau, John Burroughs, Philip Gilbert Hamerton, John Muir, John C. Van Dyke, and W. C. Bartlett have studied Nature in the trees, grasses, the birds, the animals, and the sunrises and sunsets until they have been able to thrill the world with the record of those things that they have seen and felt.

Ernest Thompson Seton, W. J. Long, and C. G. D. Roberts have studied the wild life of animals until they have written books that have charmed perhaps millions of readers by revealing to them phases of animal life that they had never believed existed.

Jack London goes up into Alaska and with trained eye observes the wild wastes of snow and winter desolation and comes back and writes books that win him fame and wealth, because of his power to see and tell what his seeing makes him feel.

This world is full of beauty, of knowledge, of joy, to the hungry mind and soul, and its treasures are all free, are all to be had merely for the asking, for the seeing, for the reaching out.

Nothing repays every effort more abundantly than does Nature. She preaches more eloquently, because more simply, purely, and directly than any divine that ever occupied pulpit. She is the direct voice of God to mankind, ordained by the Infinite himself. Few men in sacerdotal robes ever come to us with this divine song upon their lips. Joaquin Miller never wrote truer words than:

>   The woods keep repeating
>   The old sacred sermons whatever you ask.

It may be that as you read over what I have said of the observations and achievements of the scientists and others that you will say that you have no such opportunity for wide observation as this. It is not necessary that you should have. Let me suggest to you how to begin the development of your powers of observation in order that you may in your way reap as beautiful a harvest as those men have in theirs.

David was only a poor shepherd boy, but while out tending his flocks by day and night he learned the wonderful lessons that he afterwards incorporated into the Psalms. It was his observations, without scientific knowledge, without observatories, without telescopes, or other scientific instruments, that gave him such clear knowledge of the stars that he was able to sing those wonderful words that have thrilled all mankind ever since they were uttered, "The heavens declare the glory of God, and the firmament showeth His handiwork." While a shepherd boy without training, without education, he so observed the things about him that when, later in life, the power of expression came, he was able to sing messages that will live so long as man lives.

So, like David, begin to study the common things about you. Observe the flowers. Observe their loveliness. Study the infinite variety of their form, color, fragrance; compare them one with another; ask yourself why one appeals to you more than another; wherein the special beauty and attractiveness lies of one flower over another for you. No one can study the flowers and not realize that the Divine Creator loves beauty, for the infinitude of varieties that are presented, from the delicate orchids and cactuses of the tropical forests and barren deserts down to the plainest sunflower and dandelion, are all rich in a beauty and attractiveness all their own.

Ina Coolbrith, the California poet, in one of her sweetest songs, says:

> I will out in the gold of the blossoming mould
> And sit at the Master's feet,
> And the love my heart would speak,
> I will fold in the lily's rim,
> That the lips of the blossom more pure and meet
> May offer it up to Him.

See what a beautiful conception! Her heart was full of desire to lift her prayer of thankfulness, praise, and supplication up to God, but feeling her own inadequacy and incompleteness, and realizing the perfect purity of the delicate lily, she felt that she might wrap her prayer up in the rim of the flower and thus make it acceptable to the God of purity and immaculate whiteness.

There never was a flower yet that was not a miracle to the observing eye and thinking mind. How does it shape all that beauty? From whence does it gain those delicate tints, tones, and colors? From what laboratory does it extract those exquisitely delicate and delicious odors?

Oh, wake up to the beauty of the common grass, the common flowers, the common trees. Open your eyes to see, open your hearts to feel, cultivate your hunger for these common things and then absorb and assimilate them.

But the flowers and trees are but merely a part of the great world of Nature from which one may absorb things beautiful and grand.

People who live by the sea or by an inland lake have wonderful opportunities for the observation of grandeur, sublimity, and beauty. Joaquin Miller once stood by the seashore and wrote these words of poetry:

> The sun lay molten in the sea
> Of sand, and all the sea was rolled
> In one broad, bright intensity
> Of gold and gold and gold and gold.

He saw the gold of beauty which in this materialistic age few men deem of value. But when all the gold of commerce has disappeared, the gold of beauty is a treasure stored up in one's soul that will accompany him through all the ages of eternity. The one is ephemeral and useful only to provide the food, clothing, and shelter we need for the body, the other, permanent, enduring, lasting, that clothes the mind with brilliant images and the soul with helpful and stimulating aspirations.

It is one of the mistakes of life to overlook the apparently small, trifling and near-by things, in the vain desire to see some great, large, important thing. The things about us are the essential things of our life. Too often we deem them unimportant. We are so accustomed to seeing them that we pay no attention to them, yet these things were worth the thought of the Almighty Creator. Every blade of grass, every leaf of every tree is a revelation of some thought of God, hence can never be beneath the notice of mankind. This careless and unobservant attitude of mind shows our ignorance and our unwisdom. God's mysteries are before us and we refuse to read them. As Walt Whitman says: "Our streets are strewn with leaves from the book of God and we see them not." We pass them by. Let us learn to pick up these divine mysteries and in their sweet, beautiful simplicity read their sublime lessons to our own hearts.

Who would think of learning anything from the mists? Yet Joaquin Miller once wrote these words:

> Behold the silvered mists that rise
>   From all-night toiling in the corn,
>
> The mists have duties up the skies,
>   The skies have duties with the morn;
> While all the world is full of earnest care
> To make the fair world still more wondrous fair.

In one of his poems, one of our great poets tells the story of a number of poor people who came to see their king who was to approach with his gayly dressed bands of music and all the pomp and ceremony attendant upon kingship. The story goes, however, that the Captain of the Province drove the poor people away and refused to allow them to be present when the king passed through.

Let the poet now tell his own story:

> Lo, then a soft-voiced stranger said:
>   "Come ye with me a little space.
> I know where torches gold and red
>   Gleam down a peaceful, ample place;
> Where song and perfume fill the restful air,
> And men speak scarce at all. The King is there."
>
> They passed; they sat a grass-set hill—
>   What king hath carpets like to this?
> What king hath music like the thrill
>   Of crickets 'mid these silences—
> These perfumed silences, that rest upon
> The soul like sunlight on a hill at dawn?

Behold what blessings in the air!
    What benedictions in the dew!
These olives lift their arms in prayer;
    They turn their leaves, God reads them through;
Yon lilies where the falling water sings
Are fairer-robed than choristers of kings.

Lift now your heads! yon golden bars
    That build the porch of heaven, seas
Of silver-sailing golden stars—
    Yea, these are yours, and all of these!
For yonder king hath never yet been told
Of silver seas that sail these ships of gold.

They turned, they raised their heads on high;
    They saw, the first time saw and knew,
The awful glories of the sky,
    The benedictions of the dew;
And from that day His poor were richer far
Than all such kings as keep where follies are.

Have you experienced these blessings in the air? Have you felt these benedictions in the dew? Have you seen the exquisite robes of the lilies? Have you seen the ships of gold sailing through the silver seas? And the bars of gold that build the porch of heaven?

You have rushed to see the pomp of kings. You have rushed to see the glitter and tinsel of the circus procession. You have struggled with desperation that you and your wife might mingle with the gayly dressed throng at some fanciful revel. Why be so eager for these vain shows and yet not see the true beauty, real gorgeousness, undying splendor of these other outward manifestations of the thoughts of God?

Eager desire for the vain pomp and circumstance of things reveals the abnormal and depraved appetite just the same as the glutton's and drunkard's cravings do. The more they are fed the more fiercely their fires rage and the less satisfied one becomes. It is only real things that will satisfy the hunger of the immortal soul, and then one of the remarkable things is how the trivial and small things will produce satisfaction.

As George Macdonald says in his fascinating story, *Sir Gibbie*:

> It is wonderful upon how little those rare natures capable of making the most of things will live and thrive. There is a great deal more to be got out of things than is generally got out of them, whether the thing be a chapter of the Bible or a yellow turnip, and the marvel is that those who use the most material should so often be those that show the least result in strength or character.

www.ingramcontent.com/pod-product-compliance
Lightning Source LLC
Chambersburg PA
CBHW081110080526
44587CB00021B/3533